JEFFRY A. TIMMONS

The Entrepreneurial Mind

BRICK HOUSE PUBLISHING COMPANY
Andover Massachusetts

Library of Congress Cataloging-in-Publication Data
Timmons, Jeffry A.
    The entrepreneurial mind.

    Bibliography: p.
    Includes index.
    1. Entrepreneurship.   I. Title
HB615.T56   1989   338'.04   88-22301
ISBN 0-931790-84-0
ISBN 0-931790-85-9 (pbk.)

Dedication

To the **Academy of Distiguished Entrepreneurs** at Babson College (1977–1988). The combined sales of the companies they have founded or built would *equal the gross national product of the twentieth largest country in the world*:

Wally Amos, The Famous Amos Corporation
Henry W. Bloch, H & R Block, Inc.
Donald C. Burr, People Express
Nolan K. Bushnell, founder, Atari Corporation
Godtfred Kirk Christiansen, LEGO Group World Wide
Gustavo A. Cisneros, Organizacion Diego Cisneros
Trammell Crow, Trammell Crow Company
John J. Cullinane, Cullinet Software, Inc.
Thomas Mellon Evans, Crane Company
Berry Gordy, Motown Industries
J. Peter Grace, W.R. Grace & Company
Frederic C. Hamilton, Hamilton Brothers Petroleum
    Corporation
John K. Hansen, Winnebago Industries
Soichiro Honda, Honda Motor Car Company, Ltd.
Mary Hudson, Hudson Oil Company
Kazuo Inamori, Kyocera Corporation
John H. Johnson, Johnson Publishing Company, Inc.
John Erik Jonsson, Texas Instruments, Inc.
The late Ray A. Kroc, McDonald's Corporation
Mary Wells Lawrence, Wells, Rich, Greene, Inc.
Byung-Chull Lee, Samsung Group
Lewis E. Lehrman, Rite Aid Corporation
Royal Little, Textron, Inc.
Edward Lowe, Edward Lowe Enterprises, Inc.

J. Willard Marriott, Jr., Marriott Corporation

Rupert Murdoch, News America Publishing, Inc.

The late Heinz Nixdorf, Nixdorf Computer, AG

William C. Norris, Control Data Corporation

Kenneth H. Olsen, Digital Equipment Corporation

Franklin P. Perdue, Perdue Farms, Inc.

Ueli Prager, Movenpick Holding

The late Sidney R. Rabb, The Stop & Shop Companies, Inc.

Frederick W. Smith, Federal Express Corporation

Carl G. Sontheimer, Cuisinarts, Inc.

Peter J. Sprague, National Semiconductor Corporation

Sir John Marks Templeton, Templeton International

Gilbert Trigano, Club Mediterranee, S.A.

Diane Von Furstenberg, DVF, Inc.

The late Marcus Wallenberg, Skandinaviska-Enskilda
    Banken

An Wang, Wang Laboratories, Inc.

Contents

Foreword

It is rare that I can truthfully say of a book, "I couldn't put it down." Even rarer, when it is a professional book. However, Jeff Timmons has managed a refreshing, easily understood work that will be of great value to the incipient entrepreneur, and which he can read in a long evening.

The Entrepreneurial Mind reads easily, I suspect, because it supports so many of my own beliefs and prejudices about starting companies. Moreover, Timmons is a graceful and erudite writer, and has the enormous advantage of immediate familiarity with most of the studies, articles and academic research going on in the field. His ability to draw upon this knowlege, as well as nearly thirty years of experience in this field give his work an immediacy and credibility that is, I believe, unmatched anywhere.

As a distillation of what the author knows and believes about the process, the book would be a success; its real value, however, will be to the potential entrepreneur and all the Walter Mittys who dream of starting a business but lack the slightest understanding of what it really takes.

One of the book's significant contributions to the literature is the section on entrepreneurial management, wherein the skills needed to succeed in a start-up are examined and contrasted to what most managers learn at business school or working for big companies.

What makes the book enjoyable to read is of course the war stories and studies cited so generously, as well as the pungent quotations from many of our age's entrepreneur-totems, such as Ken Fisher, Famous (Wally) Amos, An Wang and many others.

This is my nominee for Top Entrepreneurship Book of 1988.

Gordon Baty

Gordon Baty *has been for over twenty years an accomplished entrepreneur, venture capitalist and author. He was the founder, president and CEO of two successful technology-based firms, subsequently acquired by Burroughs Corporation and USM Corporation. He later became founding general partner of two Boston venture-capital firms, Zero Stage Capital and First Stage Capital, which specialize in investing in seed, start-up and early-stage ventures. He has been active in the MIT Enterprise Forum, and has taught entrepreneurship at Boston-area universities. He received his S.B., S.M. and Ph.D. degrees from MIT.*

Preface

Among the adult working population in the United States about one in eight is self-employed, and it can be said that a cultural imperative exists in the minds of millions of other Americans: the entrepreneurial dream of self-employment, or starting, growing and cashing in a business. The vast majority of the two million "millionaires" in the United States have accumulated their wealth in this way.

And it is no wonder that so many have the dream, once you discover how the self-employed feel about themselves, what their work lives are like, and the economic rewards they earn. Uniformly, the self-employed report the highest levels of personal satisfaction, challenge, pride and remuneration. They love their work because it is invigorating, energizing and meaningful. They seem to love the "entrepreneurial game" for its own sake.

The rebirth of the entrepreneurial spirit in America in the past decade has brought unprecedented benefits, not just to individuals but to society as a whole. Consider the following:

- About 1.3 million new enterprises were launched in the United States in 1988.
- Virtually all of the net new jobs created in the country come from new and expanding firms—not from large, established companies. [1]

1 From 1984 to 1987, the top 5% of all *new* companies accounted for 87% of *all* new jobs, while the top 10% created 96% and the top 15% created 98%. From 1980 to 1987, the Fortune 500 eliminated a net 3.1 million people from their payrolls. At the same time, the non-Fortune 500 firms—predominately new and smaller firms—created 17 million new jobs, and the public sector contributed 1.3 million.

- Since World War II virtually all radical innovations and half of all innovations have come from new and smaller firms: the microcomputer, overnight express packages, the quick oil change, fast food, the oral contraceptive, the x-ray machine, and hundreds of others.

- Just thirty-seven individual entrepreneurs have created and/or built companies—many from nothing—to combined sales which would place their companies as the *20th largest country* (by GNP) *in the world.* Their names are entrepreneurial legends: Royal Little, An Wang, Frank Perdue, Ken Olsen, Sochio Honda, Ray Kroc, Fred Smith, Nolan Bushnell, Trammel Crow, Willard Marriott, Ed Lowe, Wally Amos, H.R. Block, Don Burr, John Cullinane, Rupert Murdoch, Peter Sprague, John Templeton—and others with equal deeds but lesser familiarity.

- Over 400 colleges and universities offer courses in new ventures and entrepreneurship, compared to as few as 50 in 1975.

- Between $50 and $60 billion of informal risk capital exists in our economy, almost entirely coming from self-made entrepreneurs.

- Another $30 billion of venture capital funds are available from professional sources seeking to back small company entrepreneurs with big ambitions—Apple Computer, Federal Express, Lotus 1-2-3, DEC, Data General, and the like started with just such sources. Such funds are now a worldwide phenomenon, including the United Kingdom, Scandanavia, Western Europe, Spain, Kenya, Brazil, Australia, Philippines, Japan, Korea, and others.

- A recent Salzburg, Austria, seminar entitled Entrepreneurship was attended by forty-six senior policy makers, researchers, entrepreneurs and executives from twenty-six countries, including Austria, Belgium, China, Egypt, England, Greece, Ireland, Malaysia, Netherlands, Norway, Poland, Portugal, Romania, Russia, Scotland, Singapore, Spain, Sweden, Turkey, West Germany and Yugoslavia. Only three of the attendees were American.

- In the United States, a recent national survey found two significant trends: (1) Women are questioning the traditional world of work and seeking alternatives to it. How? By exploring opportunities for entrepreneurship, independence and flexibility. (2) People in their fifties and sixties are not planning to retire. Many are planning on second careers, in smaller and more entrepreneurial settings.

- Entrepreneurship is not just the domain of new and small firms. It can also happen in old and large companies (though less frequently), in slower growing and even troubled companies, in profit-seeking and non-profit organizations, and in the eastern, western and developing economies.

These sources of economic progress are now being discovered worldwide and show unprecedented promise of a sustained, global entrepreneurial effort. Lighting the flame of the entrepreneurial spirit empowers nations and people with "the knowledge and ability to fish, rather than just giving them a fish."

The Entrepreneurial Mind addresses what makes entrepreneurs tick and what they do—and avoid doing—to get the odds of success in their favor. How do they convert their dreams to tangible visions and to commercial realities? What do successful entrepreneurs do differently that enables them not only to survive but to "grow up big"? How do these entrepreneurs think and act? What are their winning strategies and approaches? How do they do their homework? What do they pay a lot of attention to—and know they can ignore?

The answers to these questions unlock part of the mystery—and mythology—of entrepreneurship. Once you know how winning entrepreneurs think, act and perform, you can establish goals to practice emulating those actions, attitudes, habits and strategies—and consider in a more intelligent way if the loneliness of the entrepreneurial life is for you.

The book asks you to think of the process as a coach would in preparing for a winning season: What are the real talents, strengths and weaknesses of each player, and how can these best be exploited? What are the capabilities and shortcomings of the competition? What are the opportunities to use our strengths and capitalize on their weaknesses? Which players have to strengthen or stretch which muscles? Which moves and plays need to be practiced and executed with precision? How can we improve our stamina, and mental and physical health? Do we have players whose skills complement each others and who can play well together?

This book focuses on the founders of new ventures. It presents the knowledge and tools entrepreneurs need to analyze the risks and trade-offs of taking the start-up plunge, determining if they need a management team and how to put one together, and assessing and shaping a personal entrepreneurial strategy.

The entrepreneurial manager is another focus. What are the distinctions and the overlaps between the entrepreneurial and administrative domains? What do entrepreneurial managers need to know to start, to survive and to grow? What competencies must they have? What is unique to the task of managing rapid growth? Can entrepreneurial management be practiced *within* the large corporation?

A start-up team is necessary to build a business of any size and significant rate of growth. Over half the teams formed end in divorce in the first five years, usually destroying or crippling the venture along the way. What are the issues that need to be considered, what are the traps, how will ownership be divided, and how can these matters be addressed—in advance and along the way?

To aid the would-be entrepreneur in assessing his abilities to manage a fast-growing venture firm, various self-assessment and management competency inventories are included in the book.

This book offers a wealth of new information drawn from the venture capital industry and from research. Finally, it has been enriched by the many students exposed to it in the classroom who went forth to start their own businesses. The consensus of real-world entrepreneurs, investors and students about the material in the book is: it works!

Since 1971, and earlier doing doctoral research at the Harvard Business School, I have been immersed in the world of entrepreneurs and the start-up, development and financing of new and growing (and sometimes shrinking) companies as a student, researcher, teacher and scholar, and as an investor, advisor, director and founding shareholder. As a product of such experience, this book and the two that follow it are rooted in both real-world application and several years of refinement in classrooms and new venture workshops.

The Entrepreneurial Mind is the first of three books, which include *New Business Opportunities* and *Planning and Financing the New Venture.* The content and material have won accolades from experienced MBAs, college seniors and hundreds of founders and owners of new and emerging companies.

Much of what is here has been tempered and enhanced by my working directly with these entrepreneurs and entrepreneurial firms—usually while risking both my reputation and my wallet.

Jeffry A. Timmons
Harvard, Massachusetts
September 1988

About the Author

Jeffry A. Timmons is nationally and internationally known for his work in new ventures, venture capital, venture financing and entrepreneurship. He is currently the first holder of the Frederic C. Hamilton Professorship of Free Enterprise Development at Babson College, in Wellesley, Massachusetts. In 1989 he will become the first to hold the Class of 1954 Professorship of New Ventures and Entrepreneurship at the Harvard Business School, and will begin a joint appointment to continue his work in entrepreneurship.

He joined Babson in 1982, as Paul T. Babson Professor, and has served as Director of the Center for Entrepreneurial Studies and the Price-Babson College Fellows Program. He has conducted research, developed and teaches courses on starting new ventures and financing entrepreneurial ventures, and conducts the Entrepreneurial Management Program for the presidents and executives of emerging businesses.

Through his own consulting firm, Curtis-Palmer & Company, Inc., which he founded in 1981, his clientele have included presidents and partners of venture capital firms and emerging companies in the U.S., U.K. and Sweden, including Venture Founders Corporation and VFC Ltd, Zero Stage Capital, Investkontakt & Svetab, Venture Economics (publisher of *Venture Capital Journal*), Vlasic Foods (part of Campbell Soup Company) and The Sunmark Companies, a $160 million-plus private firm in St. Louis.

In 1971 he became a founding shareholder of Venture Founders Corporation, a Boston venture capital firm with subsidiaries in the U.K. and Belgium, with over $65 million under management. He worked closely with VFC from 1971 to 1982 in developing ways to identify, evaluate and finance seed-stage and stage-up ventures, an important testing ground for applying and refining his approaches to launching and growing higher potential ventures. Of particular note is that these investing activities have spanned a range of high, low, and no technology businesses, and product and service businesses in the U.S., Canada, U.K. and Europe. In 1981–82 he accepted a full-time assignment in Stockholm with one of the first venture capital firms there.

In 1984 as the first outside member of the partnership committee of Cellular One in Boston, he became actively involved in starting and building the first independent car phone company in New England.

In 1987 he became a founding shareholder and director of Boston Communications Group (BCG), which owns and operates Cellular One car phone systems in southern Maine and New Hampshire, and cellular phone installation and service centers.

Since 1985 he has assisted Ernst & Whinney's national Privately Owned Emerging Business Group to develop and implement professional development programs for partners in this leading Big Eight accounting firm, including Emerging Businesses and Entrepreneurship, and Financing Alternatives. This effort is now expanding to E&W International in a similar effort for the United Kingdom.

In 1988 he joined the Advisory Board of Bridge Capital Investors, a $150 million bridge fund in Teaneck, New Jersey, which specializes in providing growth capital for emerging companies with sales in the $5–100 million range.

In addition to the practical experience noted above, he has conducted research in entrepreneurship on new and emerging firms and venture financing, which has resulted in nearly one hundred papers and articles in such publications as *Harvard Business Review* and *Journal of Business Venturing,* and in the proceedings of national and international conferences, including *Frontiers of Entrepreneurship Research* (1981–87).

He is also quoted frequently in such publications as *Wall Street Journal, INC., Venture, Business Week, Entrepreneur, In Business, The New York Times, The Boston Globe, Los Angeles Times,* and elsewhere. He has authored and co-authored several books, including *New Venture Creation* (Irwin 1985), *The Encyclopedia of Small Business Resources* (Harper & Row 1984), *The Insider's Guide to Small Business Resources* (Doubleday 1982), *A Region's Struggling Savior* (SBA 1980); and has co-edited three years of *Frontiers in Entrepreneurship Research* (Babson College, 1983, 1984 and 1985).

His speaking and consulting assignments have included travels throughout the U.S., and Austria, Australia, Canada, Philippines, U.K., Scandanavia, Spain, and elsewhere.

Acknowledgements

There are many people from whom I have drawn intellectual capital and have received support and encouragement as well as inspiration. To list them all might well comprise a chapter by itself. Short of that, I wish to express special thanks to those who have been so helpful in recent years. First, my colleagues at Babson College, who have been a constant source of encourgement and friendship: Bill Bygrave, Neil Churchill, Jeff Ellis, Dan Muzyka, Ned Goodhue, Natalie Taylor, and Bill Wetzel. Also Allan Cohen, Mel Copen, Bill Dill, J.B. Kassarjian, Gordon Pritchett, and our Price-Babson College Fellows Stan Rich, Chuck Schmidt, and Randy Wise, and especially Les Charm for his generous giving of time, energy and resources to Babson.

Outside Babson, several key people have given more to this effort than they shall ever know. First, my dear friend and colleague Professor Howard H. Stevenson of the Harvard Business School stands alone for his support and for his generous sharing of ideas and extraordinary wit. Second, Paul J. Tobin, President of Cellular One and the Boston Communications Group, has been a model entrepreneur and entrepreneurial manager in pioneering (along with a superb team) the in-car telephone industry in America. I learn new lessons on entrepreneurial creativity each time I work with P.J. and see him in action. Harold Price, Gloria Appel and the late Edward Appel of the Price Institute have been unwavering champions of entrepreneurship at Babson College and across America. Their pioneering support of the Price-Babson Fellows Program has made a major contribution to helping develop entrepreneurial minds—in both faculty and students—at colleges and universities worldwide.

Hal Seigle, retired Chairman of The Sunmark Companies, St. Louis, and now a professional director and advisor to growing companies, has taught me a great deal about the difference between working hard and working smart. The inspiring example of Jake and Diana Bishop continually reminds me of Casey Stengel's advice: "They say it can't be done. But that don't always work!"

My colleagues at Ernst & Whinney's national office in the Privately Owned Emerging Business Group—Herb Braun, Gary Dando, Gyle Goodman, Bruce Mantia, and Dale Sander, in Cleveland, and partners Ron Deigleman, Dick Hadrill, Karl Mayhall, Dick Nigon, Ralph Sabin, Hy Shweil—have shown me a new perspective on how a very large firm can also be entrepreneurial.

A great debt is perpetually due all my former students, especially Peter Altman, Jeff Brown, Everett Dowling, Carl Hedberg, Greg Hunter, Jody Kosinski, Greg Murphy, Gerry Peterson, Steve Richards, and Jim Turner, from whom I learn with each encounter and marvel both at their accomplishments and how little damage I imparted!

Finally, a special thanks is due Robert Runck, President of Brick House Publishing Company, whose unique entrepreneurial nose for opportunity was instrumental in making this book possible. His creative approach to publishing ventures, and his excellent editorial wisdom and talent is evident throughout. Without his energy, effort and contributions the book would never have been written. He is also living proof why smaller, entrepreneurial publishers can succeed in the land of the giants.

Jeffry A. Timmons

What is Entrepreneurship?

Entrepreneurship is the ability to create and build something from practically nothing. It is initiating, doing, achieving, and building an enterprise or organization, rather than just watching, analyzing or describing one. It is the knack for sensing an opportunity where others see chaos, contradiction and confusion. It is the ability to build a "founding team" to complement your own skills and talents. It is the know-how to find, marshal and control resources (often owned by others) and to make sure you don't run out of money when you need it most. Finally, it is a willingness to take calculated risks, both personal and financial—and then do everything possible to get the odds in your favor.

Entrepreneurs work hard, driven by an intense commitment and determined perseverance. They burn with the competitive desire to excel and win. They use failure as a tool for learning, and would rather be effective than perfect. They respond to setbacks and defeats as if they were temporary interruptions, and rely on resiliency and resourcefulness to rebound and succeed. They have enough confidence in themselves to believe they can personally make a decisive difference in the final outcome of their ventures, and in their lives.

Creating a new venture is not a spectator sport. Its winning strategies require intense, active and creative involvement. It is a sport of challenge, uncertainty, calculated risk-taking and risk-minimizing. It parallels other activities with similar demands and unknowns. Take for instance the unknowns and urgency to act faced by the first airplane test pilot to probe the outer edge of "the performance envelope," the legendary Chuck Yeager:

... in the thin air at the edge of space, where the stars and the moon came out at noon, in an atmosphere so thin that the ordinary laws of aerodynamics no longer applied and a plane could skid into a flat spin like a cereal bowl on a waxed Formica counter and then start tumbling, end over end like a brick ... you had to be "afraid to panic." In the skids, the tumbles, the spins there was only one thing you could let yourself think about: What do I do next? [1]

The successful entrepreneurial act also can remind you of the improvisation and resourcefulness of the star football running back. Or the blitz of the downhill ski racer, speeding like a projectile, always at the precipice of disaster, but just as close to victory. The balance shifts to victory if your talents and abilities exceed the competition, and if your judgments and mental calculations result in actions that keep you pointed toward victory. And as for a downhill racer, for an entrepreneur disaster can pounce with unexpected suddenness—just ask Adam Osborne, who started a flourishing business assembling and selling a low-cost personal computer. He made a wrong move at the wrong time and his computer company is now out of business.

Still others have likened the talents of successful entrepreneurs for combining and blending people with diverse skills and personalities—so that the whole is greater than the sum of the parts—to the mastery and balancing of the symphony conductor. Or to the adroitness under stress and pressure of the skillful juggler: keeping many balls in the air at once, and invariably recovering quickly from the slightest miscue. There is a lot in common between these demanding activities and the challenges, rewards, excitement and pain that entrepreneurs face.

1 Tom Wolfe, *The Right Stuff*, 1980, pp. 51-52.

All these acts are artistic and creative. Their outcomes also tend to be either highly rewarding successes or painful and visible misses. And common to all of these is that stark urgency to act: What do I do next?

The Odds on Success

Judging by the extraordinary variety of people, opportunities and strategies which characterize the approximately 18 million (nonfarm) businesses in this country, literally anyone can give starting a business a try. Not only can they try, they can and have succeeded beyond what anyone imagined beforehand. And if they fail, no other country in the world has laws, institutions and social norms more forgiving, and that offer a second—or third—chance.

A certain level of failure is part of the dynamics of innovation and renewal in our national economy. It is also part of the learning process of an entrepreneurial apprenticeship: The failure of a single venture does not mean a career failure. To the entrepreneur, failure often serves as the flame which tempers the steel of perseverance.

The rigors of starting a business may favor the young—Nolan Bushnell, founder of Atari, Pizza Time Theaters and now Catalyst, an early stage venture-capital firm, asserts that "if you are not a millionaire or bankrupt by the time you are 30 you are not really trying!"—but age is no barrier. Just look at Colonel Sanders, who started Kentucky Fried Chicken with his first Social Security check!

Yet, while anyone can try to start a business, relatively few can grow one to beyond $1 million in sales. According to government data, only about 1 in 30 of those 18 million businesses had annual sales of over $1 million. Trying to start a venture, and growing and harvesting it successfully, are not the same. As George Bernard Shaw said, in a slightly different context, "Any darned fool can start a love affair, but it takes a real genius to end one successfully."

No doubt about it: for the vast majority of new businesses in the country, the odds against survival are high, and the odds of really making it big are very slim. For instance, fewer than five percent of all proposals to raise venture capital actually receive funding. Of those funded, fewer than ten percent become "home runs." Despite these problems, there has been an unprecedented number of new company formations in the U.S. in the past few years. Many believe that the total number of new businesses exceeds a million each year.

What happens to these new ventures? For every three new businesses formed, two close their doors. Some types of business seem to face worse odds than others. Retail trade, construction and service businesses, for instance, account for just three of twenty-one categories reported by Dun & Bradstreet, yet they account for 70% of all failures and bankruptcies.

Newness is another factor. For instance, over 53% of all business failures and bankruptcies occur in the first five years of a new firm's life; nearly 30% in years six through ten; and the remaining 20% for firms in existence more than ten years. [2] What is worse, smaller firms suffer the most. Virtually all businesses filing for bankruptcy employ fewer than 100 persons.

2 *The State of Small Business: A Report of the President*, Transmitted to the Congress, March 1983, SBA;   Dun & Bradstreet, Business Economics Division, *The Business Failure Record*, 1980;   Albert N. Shapero and Joseph Giglierano, "Exits and Entries: A Study in Yellow Pages Journalism," *Frontiers of Entrepreneurship Research 1982*, K. Vesper, ed., Babson College, Wellesley, Massachusetts.

The Right Size for Success

There appears to be a minimum size new firms attain—at least ten employees, and twenty is even better—which is closely linked both to survival odds and the promise of expansion. Translated into annual sales, this threshold is roughly $500,000. (Obviously, any estimates based on sales per employee vary considerably from industry to industry. A useful rule of thumb used here is $50,000 to $60,000 of sales per employee annually.) [3]

Much below $500,000 in sales after a few years in the business tends to mean you are fragile and vulnerable to competition, or you may not have focused on real opportunities. It may also mean you don't want to pursue them—that you have found a highly profitable but small niche in the market. A $200,000 profit on sales of $500,000 in a personal service business is the same profit earned from a supermarket with sales of $15 million! You may have personal values and lifestyle goals that conflict with the level of commitment necessary to grow a substantial venture. Or you simply are not good enough.

Another message is clear: survival odds, and signs of prosperity—namely significant job creation—improve even further once the $1 million in sales level is attained. So if you are thinking about creating a new venture with the survival odds in your favor, think big enough. Thinking small may stack the deck against you.

---

3   See David L. Birch and Susan MacCracken, "Corporation Evolution: A Micro-Based Analysis," prepared for the SBA by MIT, January 1981; Michael B. Teitz, et al., "Small Business and Employment Growth in California," Working paper No. 348, University of California, Berkeley, March 1981; and Catherine Armington and Marjorie Odle, "Small Business—How Many Jobs," *Brookings Review*, Winter 1982.

Getting the Odds to Favor Success

Fortunately, the record of new business failure has a notable pattern of exceptions to the national averages: just the opposite results characterize the failure record for entrepreneurs who are able to attract start-up financing from private venture-capital companies. Instead of a 70% to 90% *failure* rate, when all types of new firms are considered, these growth-minded new ventures enjoy a *survival* rate nearly that high. Typically, an experienced and professional venture-capital firm will lose all of the original investment in only about 15% to 20% of their companies. It is unusual for that loss rate to exceed 35%, or to fall below 10%.

What is going on here? What do these talented entrepreneurs and their venture capital backers do differently? What accounts for this exceptional record? Are there some lessons here for aspiring entrepreneurs? Clearly, these firms are carefully selected for success potential. There are vital lessons in the selection process for would-be entrepreneurs.

There are almost as many different approaches, philosophies, and nuances to the art of creating a new venture as there are venture capital companies and entrepreneurs. Yet, time and again, some central themes rise to the surface. And they are not the monopoly of entrepreneurs backed by venture capital.

A similar pattern of exceptions is evident among the *INC.* magazine top 500 firms. Of the 1 million new firms started each year, 10–12% grow less than 20% and 4% less than 40%. The average growth for the *INC.* 500 is 79%—and the majority of them have become highly successful without venture capital.

Take, for instance, Tony and Susan Harnett. Tony came to this country from his native Ireland as a young high school dropout. He had a lot of ambition and was in search of opportunity. In 1976 he and his wife bought a small natural foods store in Brookline, Massachusetts, with annual sales of $110,000 per year. By paying a lot of attention to the critical driving forces that venture capitalists seem to concentrate on, they have built Bread & Circus into a multi-store venture whose annual sales exceed $16 million. And they did this without having to raise a dime of venture capital.

What do entrepreneurs who succeed do differently? What do they know and do in pursuing opportunities and resources that make the difference? These are the questions addressed in this book.

1

The Elements of Success:
Start-ups and Early Growth

There are three primary driving forces behind successful new venture creation—a founding team, opportunity, and the necessary resources. Experience shows that these elements actually can be assessed and influenced, in order to improve the chances of succeeding. The key is a careful and realistic assessment of your strengths and weaknesses, of the opportunity, and of what is needed for success and harvest. It is an iterative, trial-and-error process of finding out what it takes, the "gaps" you face as the venture unfolds, and how to shape a good "fit." Not surprisingly, this seems to work well for a lot of innovative undertakings. After all, the Wright brothers flew over one thousand glider flights in their trial-and-error efforts to find out what worked before attaching a motor-driven propellor to their airplane.

The Founders and the Team

To a venture capitalist, what are the most important factors in succeeding with a new business? They are the lead entrepreneur and the quality of the management team. Even to those backing the most highly innovative technological ventures, where one would expect the elegance of the technology and idea to have special importance, this is true.

A good example is the philosophy of T. A. Associates, a Boston-based venture capital firm. It is one of the largest and most successful firms, with over $800 million under management and investments in over 100 emerging companies, including such winners as Biogen, Continental Cablevision, Federal Express, and Tandon. Their strong preference for high-quality management is stated this way:

The management team must have quality, depth and maturity. It must be experienced in the industry in which the company competes. The top manager should have had prior profit center responsibility. Management must possess intimate knowledge of the market for its products and have a well thought out strategy for the penetration of this market. The strength of the management team is the most important consideration in the investment decision.

Successful lead entrepreneurs and their management teams serve an "apprenticeship" of preparation, entry strategies, and planning and managing the process. Most successful entrepreneurs do not leave this to accident or osmosis. The career paths of entrepreneurs and the self-employed suggest that success is linked to thoughtful preparation and planning before taking the plunge.

There is no more powerful teacher than a good example. Seeing what has and can be done points the way cleanly and simply, and plants the seed of what is possible. There is a connection between the presence of role models and the emergence of entrepreneurs that dispels the notion of entrepreneurs being "born, not made." For instance, over half the starters of new businesses had parents who owned a business.

People who start companies are more likely to come from families in which their parents or close relatives were in business for themselves. These older people were examples or "models" for the children. Whether they were successful or not probably didn't mat-

ter. However, for the children growing up in such a family, the action of starting a new business seems possible—something they can do. [1]

The role of experience and know-how in successful venture creation is central. Ninety percent or more of founders start their companies in the same marketplace and industry they have been working in. What are the management skills and competencies necessary for the venture? How do they fit with your own strengths and weaknesses, based on your cumulative experience and track record? How do your skills complement those of possible partners? What are some effective and time-saving ways to get the experience you need? Some attitudes and actions can in fact be acquired and learned, and some are more desirable than others. [2] In the end, it is what you do that counts.

Since successful entrepreneurs seem to come in as many sizes, shapes, colors and descriptions as is imaginable, there doesn't seem to be one single profile or psychological model. Rather, what is vital is the blend and fit among the founding team. Is there a talented lead entrepreneur whose capabilities are complemented by equally committed partners? Can they work together effectively? Are their collective know-how

1 Arnold Cooper and William Dunkelberg, "A New Look at Business Entry," NIFB, March, 1984.

2 Karl H. Vesper, "New Venture Ideas: Don't Overlook the Experience Factor," *Harvard Business Review*, May-June 1980. Robert H. Brockhaus, "The Psychology of the Entrepreneur," Chapter 3, *Encyclopedia of Entrepreneurship*, Kent, Sexton and Vesper, eds., Prentice-Hall, 1982, pp. 50-55. J. A. Timmons, "Careful Self-Analysis and Team Assessment Can Aid Entrepreneurs," *Harvard Business Review*, Nov-Dec 1979.

and capacities the critical ones necessary to seize and execute the opportunity? If the answers are "yes" to these questions, then there is a good fit, and the chances for success are dramatically improved.

Finally, there are some issues more elusive and tougher to define: personal attitudes and philosophy, values and ethics. There appear to be some important attitudes and values that successful entrepreneurs share. They see the cup as half-full, rather than half-empty. They ask, "How can I make it work?" rather than dwelling on why it won't work. Their beliefs can include such notions as "Bite off more than you can chew, and then chew it" (Roger Babson); "You can do anything you want to do" (Wally Amos, Famous Amos Chocolate Chip Cookies); "You need ... to think yourself out of a corner, meet needs, and never, never accept no for an answer" (John Johnson, EBONY); "Never give up" (Carl Sontheimer, Cuisinart). The vital importance of developing such attitudes and perseverance is an essential part of the entrepreneurial mind-set. [3]

Without a team it is extremely difficult to raise venture capital. As was noted earlier, it is now well established that most experienced investors consider a proven management team to be the most critical ingredient of start-up success.

A team is equally important to the chances of survival *and expansion* in new ventures, whether or not those ventures are candidates for invested capital. It was earlier mentioned that those firms who managed to grow beyond 20

3 See the excellent summary of a study of the first twenty-one inductees into Babson College's Academy of Distinguished Entrepreneurs, by John A. Hornaday and Nancy Tieken, "Capturing Twenty-One Heffalumps," in *Frontiers of Entrepreneurship Research 1983*, Hornaday, Timmons and Vesper, eds.; Babson College, Wellesley, Massachusetts, pp. 23-50.

employees or roughly $1 million in sales were less likely to fail than most. In a large majority of businesses it is quite difficult to do this without a team of at least two key contributors.

Take, for example, the CEO of Telesis, one of the emerging high-growth firms in the CAD/CAM business. Before he was recruited by the company's venture capital backers, he was president of one of the early entrants in the office automation business, Vydec Office Systems.

At Telesis, the first key addition he made to his management team was a people specialist—his former vice president of human resources at Vydec. Contrary to some team builders, he did not begin by hiring a marketing, financial or manufacturing expert. Why was this so?

The CEO knew from his previous experience that the greatest single barrier to rapid growth is usually finding the right people, soon enough. He was anticipating this critical need about a year or two earlier than many expansion team builders do.

A final point should be made about the importance of a team for a venture experiencing growing pains. There is growing evidence that having the right partner(s) can be invaluable in coping with the high degree of loneliness and stress associated with entrepreneurship. [4]

Yet, teams are not for everyone, and they don't have to be. The purpose of highlighting the role of the team here is to drive home one message: While the heroic, individual entrepreneur may make an excellent living, it takes a team-

---

[4] David Boyd and David E. Gumpert, "Stress, Loneliness and the Entrepreneur," *Frontiers Of Entrepreneurship Research 1984*, Babson College, Wellesley, Massachusets.

oriented entrepreneur to build an organization, create value for others, and realize a capital gain.

The Opportunity

If there is a single magnet pulling out the entrepreneurial event, it is opportunity. The problem does not seem to be the lack of ideas: entrepreneurs and innovators abound with new ideas. What is the problem, then? Simply put, unsuccessful entrepreneurs usually equate an idea with an opportunity; successful entrepreneurs know the difference.

Judging by the failure statistics described earlier, it is apparent that the vast majority of entrepreneurs run out of money before they find enough customers for their "good ideas." A novel idea or invention is not the same as a sound business anchored to a marketable idea. Is there really a business opportunity, or just a product? Further, the window on the opportunity depends upon movement in technology and competitors' activities. The opportunity not only has a finite life, but is a constantly moving target.

The real challenge is recognizing an opportunity buried in the noise and chaos of the marketplace. And a skillful entrepreneur can often shape and create an opportunity where others see little or nothing. If it were simply a matter of using available evaluation methods we might have far more than the nearly a million ventures in the U.S. whose annual sales exceed $1 million. Why? Because over 200 techniques for screening and evaluating ideas have been developed and documented.

The more certain you are that you have spotted a viable window on opportunity, the more effectively you can use your time in preparing to seize it. Pulling together the essential parts of a business plan can take several weeks, sometimes months, or longer, even when you are allocating most of your time to it. Writing it down can take a hundred hours or more as you sharpen your focus. So being quite sure, before beginning to prepare a formal plan, that a real opportunity exists can save you valuable time in the end.

Knowing which opportunity to focus on and which to say "no" to is key. Equally important is knowing when you do not need or cannot afford the time necessary to prepare a full-blown business plan. There are times when the voice of experience tells you that you had better get to that window before it shuts.

Venture capitalists often see demonstrated the old adage, "one man's meat is another man's poison." Different investors will look into the same venture and come to opposite conclusions. The same is true of opportunities facing entrepreneurs. For every manager, engineer, sales or technical person who sheds the "bronze" or even "golden" handcuffs of employment to join a new venture, there are always several that do not view the opportunity as so compelling. Why is this so?

Imagine finding your opportunity on the Bering Sea, running a small outpost in Bethel, Alaska, 800 miles west of Anchorage, reachable only by sea and air. One entrepreneur went there for a job opportunity. Within two years of his arrival he bought the general store he was running. He subsequently saw even greater opportunities in salmon fishing. In 1980 he expected to gross over $5 million and earn a substantial profit.

Defining a good opportunity is obviously no easy matter. Some of the more important issues include:

• What is the competitive vacuum creating the opportunity? What are the underlying reasons for the vacuum, and can they be articulated? How long will it last?

• For whom is the opportunity desirable and do-able? The personal values and life-styles of the founders enter heavily into the definition of a good opportunity.

• Is there a market: a real need for the product or service? How does it add value for the customer? Have the customers been identified, are they reachable and are they enthusiastic?

• What are the economics of the opportunity? Are the gross margins and potential profits sufficient and durable enough to cushion errors made during the heat of start-up, and to sustain growth? How long will it take to reach a positive cash flow and break even? How much capital will be required to get there?

• Given your alternatives, do the risk-reward trade-offs work in your favor? What needs to be done to shift the balance in the direction you would like? The upside may be exceedingly attractive, but can you absorb the down side, should that occur, both in terms of dollars and psychological stress?

There are many benchmarks, analytical tools and rules of thumb used to size up an opportunity. At one end of the continuum are the highly selective criteria used by venture capitalists. At the other end might be those appropriate to small, individual businesses. Somewhere in between is a mix that is a good fit, based on your self-assessment of your goals, aspirations, experience and talents at this time.

The Business Plan

Today advice about business-plan preparation is readily available. Venture capitalists and informal, private investors (or "angels") across the country praise the high quality of the plans they are seeing. With the advent of the microcomputer and spreadsheet software, the agony factor has diminished and the time needed to prepare a plan has shortened.

Think of the business plan as the entrepreneur's "flight simulator." Developing it enables the planner to think through and practice mixing the critical ingredients of the start-up without unnecessary risk. Preparing a business plan is much more a process than a product. Doing it compresses and accelerates the learning necessary to start a company —especially if you are doing it for the first time.

Writing the business plan is the easy part (although you won't think so when you do it). It is implementation where the real work and challenge begins. What investors, bankers, customers and prospective key employees want to know is how to make it work. Having a superbly prepared plan may be a necessary but far from sufficient condition for launching and building a million-dollar-plus venture.

How important is a business plan? Without it, your chances of raising venture capital or other formal or informal financing is nearly impossible—unless, of course, you don't need it. Nolan Bushnell was once asked this question by a young woman at Babson College: "Do we really have to prepare business plans? They are a real pain. We sometimes work on one most of the semester and then find out the business will not work!" Bushnell's response was unequivocal: "Absolutely, yes. Every time you prepare a business plan you become a better entrepreneur. It is a lot of work but it is worth every bit of the effort. Do it."

The Use of Resources

Entrepreneurs seem to have a quite different mentality when it comes to resources, especially in contrast to large, established companies. In fact, the working definition of entrepreneurship is "the pursuit of opportunity without regard to resources you currently control." [5] Entrepreneurs know that they can get the odds in their favor, even improve the chances of attaining their goals, without having to own the assets and resources. They also manage to get more out of less. Their approach often is to push ahead with minimum, rather than maximum, resources. This is also a good way to reduce the early risks and exposure, while working through the trial-and-error process of finding out if there really is an opportunity and how likely it is to succeed.

Take, for instance, Howard Head's approach to developing the first metal ski. Working with his own savings, literally out of his own garage, he tried more than 40 versions before he finally developed a marketable metal ski. Head subsequently dominated the international ski industry through the late 1960s. Head is convinced that had he insisted on having all the right talent, back-up and financing in place before starting to develop the product, he would have wasted it all prematurely and failed.

Early stage entrepreneurs also position themselves so that they can control the resources, which they view as more important than owning the resources. Most large corporations are quite likely to view the situation just the opposite way, and seek to own the assets or resources.

For example, start-up entrepreneurs know they can stretch limited cash and new capital by renting or leasing new equipment, vehicles or building, instead of buying them. They will take cuts in pay in order to plow funds into growing the business. They work exceptionally hard in the

6 Definition developed by Howard Stevenson and his colleagues at the Harvard Business School.

early stages, often sixty hours or more a week, and thereby minimize the need for additional people. Once a business is on a solid footing, it often requires two or three new hires to get nearly the same results in the jobs held initially by the founders.

Finding and properly using the most helpful outsiders—banker, CPA, lawyer, informal advisors, board members, and other experts—is one of the most easily overlooked challenges start-up entrepreneurs face.

Most people include money among the top three ingredients needed to launch a new company successfully. No doubt about it, you cannot go far without it. After all, it is the fuel in the tank that makes the company go. Yet, it is included here last. Why?

Your capacity to raise money is a result of having the other parts of the act together. The financing does not *cause* these other things to happen; in most instances it *follows* good people who have spotted good opportunities, and who demonstrate that they clearly grasp the forces that will govern success.

Today there is no serious shortage of risk capital. Ironically, there continues to be more venture capital available—over $4 billion in 1987 alone—than there are new ventures with all the pieces in place. The same appears to be true of non-venture financing. Increasingly sophisticated bankers, financial institutions and informal investors back people who have demonstrated that they understand the elements needed to succeed in their proposed business.

2

The Entrepreneur

Who can be an entrepreneur, what does it take, and when and why do entrepreneurs take the plunge? What works for entrepreneurs who build businesses? Can you develop concepts and practical guides for evaluating your entrepreneurial alternatives, and for shaping an entry strategy and apprenticeship?

As recently as fifty years ago a large body of opinion held that leaders are born, not made: you either had it or you did not. The roots of much of this thinking reflect the assumptions and biases of an earlier era when rules were royal and leadership was the prerogative of the aristocracy.

Fortunately, such notions have not withstood the test of practice and time, nor the inquisitiveness of researchers. It is widely accepted now that leadership, while an extraordinarily complex subject, depends more on the connections among the leader, the task and situation, and those being led, than on inborn or inherited attributes alone.

Today, there is a similar debate surrounding the entrepreneur on the born/made issue. The evidence is mounting, however, that a good deal about becoming a successful entrepreneur can be learned, although probably not by everyone, nor from everyone. Since entrepreneurs frequently evolve from an entrepreneurial heritage, and are shaped and nurtured by their closeness to entrepreneurs and their experience, an apprenticeship can be useful. A lot of what you need to know about entrepreneuring—and whether it is really for you—comes from experience:

knowing what to prepare for, where to position yourself, and when to move on.

Should you try it? To help you decide, a series of self-assessment and goal-setting exercises are presented in this book that students and practicing entrepreneurs have found extremely valuable. As one woman, who founded a rapidly growing medical database and information company recently sold to a large pharmaceutical firm for over $5 million, put it: "Self-assessment is the hardest thing for entrepreneurs to do, but if you don't do it you will really get into trouble."

The focus in this book is on the potentially highly profitable venture aimed at an eventual capital gain. If you decide you do not want to grow and harvest a venture, then you may be better off working your way into a pair of "golden handcuffs" in a medium to large size company. Or if what you want to do is own and run a modern day mom-and-pop store—the boutique, liquor shop, corner convenience store or tourist shop—recognize that these types of ventures are really only jobs. They may support two or three people, and generate a decent living, but they are fragile and vulnerable to competition, sudden changes in the community, or the owner's boredom, and are rarely sold for a capital gain that amounts to much. As one entrepreneur summed it up: "A one-person business makes a living. It takes an organization to make money."

Characteristics of Entrepreneurs

During the past decade an unprecedented and explosive rebirth of entrepreneurship has occurred in America and across the Western world. Accompanying this trend has been a significant increase in knowledge and research about the entrepreneurial process. As the new body of knowledge about entrepreneurship continues to evolve rapidly, much of what was known previously has been reinforced and refined, some has been challenged, and numerous new insights have emerged. [1]

Growth-minded entrepreneurs possess both a creative and innovative flair *and* solid management skills and business know-how. These attributes seem to distinguish entrepreneurs from others such as inventors, promoters, managers in large, stable organizations, and bureaucratic administrators.

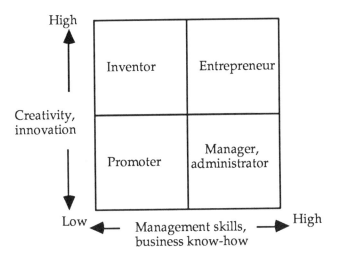

Inventors are noted for their creative genius. Untold numbers of new ideas and innovations are spawned from just such creativity. Yet most of these ideas never become commercial reality, since their inventors often lack the interest, the business/management know-how, or both.

Promoters often are quite creative in the schemes and programs they devise. But typically they mount one-shot

1   Reported in *Frontiers of Entrepreneurship Research*, edited by J. Hornaday, J. Timmons, and K. Vesper, et al., annual volumes 1981-1985, The Center for Entrepreneurial Studies, Babson College, Wellesley MA 02157.

events or propositions, with a strong bias toward the instant gratification of getting rich quickly. Serious management skills are often lacking in promoters—they do not need them, and they often lack the depth and integrity necessary for long-term success.

Managers have to develop strong managerial skills and business know-how, but they are less known for their creative and innovative solutions, especially in steady-state, slow or no-growth enterprises. More commonly, they aim for efficiency and effectiveness.

Administrators govern, police and ensure the smooth operation of the *status quo*. Their skills are tuned to efficiency. Creativity and innovation are not required, and may actually be counterproductive in bureaucratic environments.

The growth-minded entrepreneur is both creative and a capable manager. These two driving forces enable him *or* her not only to conceive and launch a business, but to make it grow and succeed. As the Chinese fortune cookie says: "To open a business, very easy. To keep it open, very difficult."

The profiles and track records of growth-minded entrepreneurs are rich in experience. While there are some outstanding exceptions, such as Steven Jobs, co-founder of Apple Computer, and Mitch Kapor, founder of Lotus Software, most founders first acquire substantial, relevant general management and sales/marketing experience. They are more likely to be over thirty than under thirty when they attract the caliber of partners and financial backers necessary to launch and grow a significant venture. They are more likely to have eight to ten years of experience (or more) than less than five.

Among technology-based ventures, the founders are usually college trained, and are quite likely to possess an advanced degree. This is not true among founders of low-technology businesses. Their prior experience is always in basically the same technology, products and markets in which they plan to launch their new company.

Major pluses in the eyes of investors and bankers are general management and marketing experience, including some favorable profit-and-loss experience. Typically, about three fourths of successful entrepreneurs have had some direct sales experience.

Growth-minded entrepreneurs are more likely to start the venture with a partner or two. They are likely to have accumulated enough net worth to contribute to the funding of the start-up entirely, or at least in some significant way. If they have not attained enough net worth, then their track records are impressive enough to give investors and creditors the necessary confidence to provide funding.

They have also identified enough reachable customers for their product or service—before they start the business—so that they can reach breakeven before they run out of start-up cash or become strong enough to attract additional capital. Finally, they usually have found and nurtured relevant business and other contacts and networks that contribute to the ultimate success of the venture.

The implications of all this are clear: one principal task for an entrepreneur is to determine what kind of an entrepreneur he or she is likely to become, based on background, experience and drive—and whether these proclivities fit with the opportunity. If they do, then the entrepreneur can shape a plan to make it happen.

Myths and Realities of Entrepreneurship

Folklore and stereotypes about entrepreneurs are remarkably durable, even in these informed and sophisticated times. Take, for instance, the following examples of myths and realities.

Myth: Entrepreneurs are born, not made. *Reality:* There is increasing evidence that successful entrepreneurs emerge from a combination of work experience, study, and development of appropriate skills. While there are no doubt attributes which you either have or you don't, possessing them does not necessarily an entrepreneur make, and other skills of equal importance can, in fact, be acquired through understanding, hard work and patience.

Myth: Anyone can start a business. It's a matter of luck and guts. All you need is a new idea; then go for it. *Reality:* If you want to launch and grow a high-potential venture you must get the odds in your favor. You cannot think and act like an inventor, or a promoter, or even a manager; you must think and act like an entrepreneur.

Myth: Entrepreneurs are gamblers. They roll the dice and take the consequences. *Reality:* Successful entrepreneurs are very careful to calculate the risks they take. They get others to share risk with them, thereby lowering their personal exposure. When they find they can avoid or minimize risks, they do so.

Myth: You are better off as an independent, lone entrepreneur, owning the whole show yourself. *Reality:* It is extremely difficult to grow a venture beyond $1 million in profitable sales working single-handedly. Ventures that succeed usually have multiple founders. Besides, one hundred percent of nothing is nothing.

Myth: Being an entrepreneur is the only way you can really be your own boss and completely independent. *Reality:*

Entrepreneurs are far from independent, and have many masters and constituencies to serve and juggle—partners, investors, customers, suppliers, creditors, employees, spouse, family and social and community obligations.

Myth: Entrepreneurs work longer and harder than managers in big companies. *Reality:* According to a recent survey of Harvard Business School alumni, a spectrum of "hours per week worked" shows that the self-employed actually work more *and* less than their corporate counterparts. [2] If you can make money for a large company, chances are you can do it for your own company.

Myth: Entrepreneurs face greater stress and more pressures, and thus pay a higher price for their role than any others. *Reality:* Being an entrepreneur is stressful and demanding. But there is no evidence that it is any more stressful than other demanding professional roles, such as a partner in a large accounting or law firm, or head of a large corporation or government agency.

Compared to managers in the Harvard study, nearly three times as many entrepreneurs said they did not plan to retire ever; almost three fourths said they would be entrepreneurs again if they had to do it all over. Most entrepreneurs enjoy what they do; they reported more fun than drudgery; they thrived on the flexibility and innovative aspects of their jobs. Other studies also show that entrepreneurs report very high job satisfaction.

Myth: Starting your own company is a risky, hazardous proposition which often ends in failure. *Reality:* Success, rather than failure, is more common among higher potential ventures because they are driven by talented and experienced founders in pursuit of attractive opportunities, who are able

2 Stevenson, "Who are the Harvard Self-Employed?" op. cit.

to attract both the right people and necessary financial and other resources to make the venture work.

Myth: Money makes the difference. If you have enough working capital you will succeed. *Reality:* Money is the least important ingredient in new venture success. If the other pieces and talents are there, the money will follow.

Money is not a prime motivator, either. Entrepreneurs thrive on the "thrill of the chase." Time and again, even after they have made a few million dollars, they still work long hours and launch more companies.

Myth: Start-ups are for the young and energetic. *Reality:* While these qualities may help, it appears that age is no barrier to a start-up, and can have advantages, such as well-developed networks of contacts. One study showed that one fifth of the founders were over forty when they embarked on their entrepreneurial career, the majority were in their thirties, and just over one-quarter did so by the time they were twenty-five. Further, numerous examples exist of start-ups whose founders were over sixty. [3]

Myth: Entrepreneurs are motivated solely by the quest for the almighty dollar; they want to make money so they can spend it. *Reality:* Growth-minded entrepreneurs are more driven by building the enterprise and realizing long-term capital gains than by instant gratification through high salaries and perks. A sense of personal achievement and accomplishment, feeling in control of their own destinies, and realizing their vision and dreams are also powerful motivators. Money is viewed as a tool and a way of keeping score.

Myth: Entrepreneurs seek power and control over others so they can feel in charge. *Reality:* While many entre-

---

3 Robert Ronstadt, *Entrepreneurship*, Lord Publishing Company, 1984.

preneurs are driven this way, most successful growth-minded entrepreneurs are just the opposite. They are driven by the quest for responsibility, achievement and results, rather than power. They thrive on a sense of accomplishment from outperforming the competition, rather than by a personal need for power expressed by dominating and controlling others. They gain control by their results.

How Long Does It Take?

It takes time to create and build any successful activity, whether it is in a new venture or in another organization. There is a saying in the venture capital business that the "lemons," or losers in a portfolio, ripen in about two and a half years. The "plums," or winners, on the other hand, usually take seven or eight years to bear fruit. It simply takes that long to get it all together to the point that a solid success is evident. Even in smaller, emerging new businesses, most founders say that it wasn't until the fourth or fifth year that they were confident that the new business would succeed.

Obviously, it can take a shorter or a longer period of time, but seven years is a realistic time frame to have in mind for growing a higher potential business to a point where a capital gain can be realized. Interestingly, the same approximate time frame of seven years is given by college and large corporation presidents, and self-employed professionals, for how long it takes to do something significant.

The implications of this time frame are quite provocative. Assume you spend the first five years after high school, a stint in the military, college or graduate school gaining the relevant experience you need. You are twenty to thirty years of age, maybe thirty-five. How many new ventures can you launch, grow and successfully harvest, thereby realizing a capital gain? By the time you are fifty you might have had time for three, assuming everything went according to schedule, which it rarely does. Of course, you do not have to stop then, but realistically the odds are you will be slowing down, whether you want to or not.

What is more, it is not uncommon for first-time entrepreneurs to go through some false starts, even a failure or two, in the trial-and-error process of learning the entrepreneurial ropes. As a result, the first high-potential venture may not be launched until you are in your mid-to-late thirties. You may grow this one, and maybe one more. Of course, there is always the possibility of staying with the venture and growing it to a larger company, say $50 million sales or more. But for many ventures, particularly where the technology, competition, marketplace, and regulatory environment—or any combination—are rapidly changing, the harvest can be missed completely.

Reflecting on all this will reveal some paradoxes and dilemmas. For one thing, just when your drive, energy and ambition are at a peak—usually in your twenties to early thirties—the necessary relevant business experience and management skills are least developed. And that critical element labeled wisdom and judgement is in its infancy. You are straining at the bit to launch and realize your dream, but you lack the experience necessary for success. Later on, when you have gained the experience, wisdom and judgement you need to focus on your entrepreneurial goals, mother nature has begun to tax the energy and drive that got you this far.

Other paradoxes are also apparent. You will need patience and perseverance relentlessly to pursue your long-term vision. But you will need to balance that with the flexibility to abandon one moving target of opportunity and shift to others.

It is fair to say that your first ten years out of school can make you or break you in terms of how well you are prepared for serious entrepreneuring. While it may never be too late, new evidence further suggests that the most durable entrepreneurial careers, those found to last 25 years or more, were begun across a broad age spectrum, but after the person selected work specifically to prepare for an entrepreneurial career. (Ibid.)

3

The Nature of Success

Winning Thoughts and Actions

There is greater value in noting what successful entrepreneurs actually do—their winning actions and behaviors—and their attitudes, than in focusing on their psychological characteristics. Besides, there is no single profile or psychological model which can accurately define and predict all entrepreneurial types, though various efforts have been made. [1]

There are common actions, approaches and attitudes of vital importance. These characteristics of success also suggest who would be good partners and key managers to complement the lead entrepreneur, and help identify which behaviors seem to work and can be nurtured and developed. The characteristics therefore have important implications for entrepreneurs, investors, creditors and prospective partners.

The first twenty-one inductees into Babson's Academy of Distinguished Entrepreneurs, including such founders as Ken Olson (DEC), An Wang (Wang Computers), Wally Amos (Famous Amos' Chocolate Chip Cookies), Bill Norris (Control Data), Soichiro Honda (Honda Motors), and the late Ray Kroc (McDonald's), all mentioned three attributes and behaviors as the principal reasons for their successes. All three can be learned:

Respond positively to challenges; learn from mistakes.

Take personal initiative.

1 Karl Vesper, *New Venture Strategies*, Prentice-Hall, 1980, Ch. 1.

Have great perseverance and determination. [2]

Time and again, entrepreneurs who are very successful argue that there are common denominators they seek in the people they want to surround themselves with to build a high potential business.

Take Ken Fisher, for example. He joined Prime Computer in 1975 as president when the company had sales of just $7 million and employed 150. In six years the company grew to $365 million in sales and 4,500 employees. Sales grew at a compounded annual rate of 88%, net income 108%, while return on shareholder's equity reached a high of 48.8% and topped 35% for four consecutive years. During his stay Prime's share price increased 126 times to its high just prior to his resignation.

He subsequently formed Encore Computer Corporation with two industry leaders. At a luncheon talk a few years ago he made it very clear that "you should look for certain traits—it works: an ego that sustains and drives a person to achieve, stress tolerance, controlled empathy, ability to resolve conflicts, keeping everything in perspective between the business and personal life, and least important of all these, intelligence." He quickly added that "we have done amazing things with people of ordinary intelligence."

What follows is a summary of the entrepreneurial mind in thought and action. Habits of thinking and acting like an entrepreneur can be valuable allies in turning venture ideas into commercial reality.

---

2 J. A. Hornaday and N. B. Tieken, "Capturing Twenty-One Heffa-lumps," in *Frontiers of Entrepreneurship Research* 1983, pp. 23-50.

Total Commitment, Determination And Perseverance.
More than any other single factor, total dedication and
perseverance to succeed as an entrepreneur can overcome
incredible obstacles and setbacks. Sheer determination, and
an unwavering commitment to succeed, will eventually win
out against odds that would defeat most people. It can also
compensate enormously for other weaknesses you may have.

Someone looking for venture capital financing can expect
investors to measure founder commitment in several ways.
Are you willing to invest a substantial portion of your net
worth in the venture, including taking out a second
mortgage on your house? Will you take a cut in pay, since
you will own a major piece of the venture? Have you made
major sacrifices in your life style, family circumstances, and
standard of living to make the venture progress far enough
to interest outside investors?

The reality is that launching and building a venture is
highly demanding and stressful, even if it does not require
venture capital to finance the launch.

Drive To Achieve and Grow.   Entrepreneurs are self-
starters, driven internally by a strong desire to compete, to
excel against self-imposed standards, and to pursue and attain
challenging goals. The competitive needs of growth-minded
entrepreneurs are to outperform their own previous results,
rather than to just outperform another person. Having an
objective way of keeping score, such as changes in profits,
sales or stock price, is also important. Thus, money is seen as
a tool, and a way of keeping score, rather than the object of
the game by itself.

Orientation to Opportunities and Goals.   One clear
pattern among successful growth-minded entrepreneurs is
their focus on opportunity rather than resources, structure or

strategy. They start with the opportunity and let their understanding of it guide their actions. Setting high but attainable goals enables them to focus their energies, be very selective in sorting out opportunities, and know what to say "no" to. Having goals and direction also helps define priorities, and provides measures of how well they are performing. It is noteworthy that the Chinese characters for crisis and problem, when combined, mean opportunity.

Taking Initiative and Personal Responsibility. The entrepreneur has historically been viewed as an independent and highly self-reliant innovator, the champion (and occasional villain) of the private enterprise economy. Modern research into the entrepreneur has confirmed some of these earlier generalizations, but has refined considerably the ways of focusing on this self-reliant attitude.

Effective entrepreneurs actively seek out and take initiative. They willingly put themselves in situations where they are personally responsible for the success or failure of the operation. They like to take the initiative to solve a problem, or fill a vacuum where no leadership exists. They also like situations where their personal impact on problems can be measured. Again, this is the action-oriented nature of the entrepreneur expressing itself. In fact, one motto of the entrepreneur might well be: "Anything worth doing is worth doing poorly, just to get it done!"

Persistence in Problem-Solving. As noted, entrepreneurs who successfully build new enterprises posses an intense level of determination and desire to overcome hurdles, solve a problem, and complete the job. They are not intimidated by difficult situations. In fact, their self-confidence and general optimism seems to translate into a view that the impossible just takes a little longer.

Yet they are neither aimless nor foolhardy in their relentless attack on a problem or obstacle which can impede their business. If the task is extremely easy or perceived to be unsolvable, the entrepreneur will actually give up sooner than others. While entrepreneurs are persistent they are also realistic in recognizing what they can and cannot do, and where they can get help to solve a very difficult but necessary task.

Veridical Awareness and Sense of Humor. The best entrepreneurs have a keen awareness of their own strengths and weaknesses, those of their partners, and the competitive and other environments surrounding and influencing them. They are realistic about what they can and cannot do, and do not delude themselves, which is the definition of "veridical awareness."

This veridical awareness, or "optimistic realism," is often accompanied by a sense of humor. The ability to retain a sense of perspective, and to "know thyself," makes it possible for an entrepreneur to laugh, to ease tensions, and frequently to get an unfavorable situation moving in a more profitable direction.

Seeking and Using Feedback. Growth-minded entrepreneurs have an insatiable desire to know how well they are performing. They realize that in order to know how well they are doing, and how to improve their performance, they need actively to seek out, digest and use feedback. This is also central to the habit of learning from mistakes and setbacks, and responding in a resilient way to the unexpected. For the same reasons, particularly good entrepreneurs are often described as excellent listeners, and quick learners.

As we will see, seeking out people to listen to and learn from has a benefit beyond that of instant feedback for the entrepreneur; it also arouses the interest of the person whose opinion is sought. In this way, the entrepreneur strengthens his or her supporting network as well as obtaining the benchmarks he or she needs.

Internal Locus of Control. Successful entrepreneurs believe in themselves. They do not believe the success or failure of their venture will be governed by fate, luck, or other powerful, external forces or persons. They believe that their accomplishments and setbacks lie within their own control and influence, that they personally can affect the outcome. This attitude is also consistent with the self-confident desire to take personal responsibility—so long as it does not lead to overconfidence, arrogance, or lack of humility.

Tolerance for Ambiguity, Stress and Uncertainty. Ask people working in a large company how sure they are that they will receive their paycheck this month, in two months, six months, and next year this time. Invariably, they will say virtually for certain, and they will muse at the question. Start-up entrepreneurs face just the opposite levels of certainty: there may be no revenue at the beginning, and if there is, a ninety day backlog would be an exception. To make matters worse, this uncertainty is compounded by the constant changes which introduce ambiguity and stress into every part of the enterprise: jobs are undefined and changing continually, customers are new, co-workers are new, setbacks and surprises are inevitable. And there never seems to be enough time. Lack of organization, structure and order is a way of life.

Entrepreneurs take all this in stride, and many would say actually thrive on the fluidity and excitement of such an ambiguous existence. Job security and retirement generally aren't of any concern to entrepreneurs. Recall the study of self-employed graduates of Harvard Business School, which showed that over 40% of them planned never to retire, while the same figure for non-entrepreneurs was about 16%.

Calculated Risk-taking and Risk-sharing.   Successful entrepreneurs are not gamblers.   Like a sky diver, they are willing to take a calculated risk.   They risk much more than money: they risk their reputations. In deciding to take the plunge, they do everything possible to get the odds in their favor, to avoid unnecessary risks.   With accumulated net worth and a successful track record, they are inclined to take even less risk: they simply do not have to, and also they have more to lose.

Their strategies also include getting others to share the risks with them: partners put money and reputations on the line, investors do likewise, creditors join the party, as do customers who advance payments, and suppliers who advance credit. And when you are just getting started in an entrepreneurial career you may have to take larger risks than after you are successful. Either way, a carefully calculated, downright cunning approach to risk-taking will serve you well.

Three very successful entrepreneurs in California "initiate and orchestrate actions which, while not risky to themselves, have risk consequences. And while they shun risk, they sustain their courage by the clarity and optimism with which they see the future. They limit the risks they initiate by carefully defining and strategizing their ends and controlling and monitoring their means—and tailoring them both to what they see the future to be. Further, they manage risk by transferring it to others." [3]

Low Need for Status and Power. Growth-minded entrepreneurs derive personal motivation from the challenge and excitement of creating and building the enterprise. They are driven by a thirst for achievement rather for status and power. Ironically, their accomplishments, especially if they are very successful, give them status and power. But it is important to recognize that power and status are a result of their activities and not the need that is propelling and motivating their actions.

Further, when a strong need for control, influence and power characterizes the lead entrepreneur, the venture usually gets into trouble. A dictatorial, adversarial and domineering management style makes it very difficult to attract and keep people who thrive on achievement, responsibility and results. Compliant partners and managers are those often chosen.

Destructive conflicts erupt over who has the final say, who is "right," and whose prerogatives will prevail. Reserved parking spaces, the corner office with the oriental rug, and the fancy automobiles become symbols of power and status, which foster a value system and culture which is not usually conducive to growth. The emphasis in such cases is no longer on the opportunity, the customer and market, and knowing the competition.

In fact, among successful entrepreneurs there is a well-developed capacity to exert influence without formal power. They are adept at conflict resolution. They know when to

---

3 Daryl Mitton, "No Money, Know-How, Know-Who: Formula for Managing Venture Success and Personal Wealth," *Frontiers of Entrepreneurship Research* 1984.

use logic and when to persuade, when to make a concession and when to exact one. In order to run a successful venture, entrepreneurs must learn to get along with many different constituencies, often with conflicting aims—the customer, the supplier, the financial backer, the creditor, as well as the partners and others on the inside. Arranging an accommodation cannot be done by a formal declaration of "Do as I say." Success comes when the entrepreneur is a mediator—a negotiator rather than a dictator.

Integrity and Reliability. Perhaps the surest way to build and insure a successful entrepreneurial career—or any other career, for that matter—is to insist on personal standards of integrity and reliability. Do what you say you are going to do. In the long haul such an approach is vital. With it the possibilities are limitless. Your opportunity tree will grow and grow beyond your fondest imagination. Why? Because it is the glue and fiber that binds successful personal and business relationships, and makes them endure. Investors, partners, customers and creditors alike value this attribute highly.

Sadly, the temptations of a short-term gain often lure too many aspiring entrepreneurs to compromise their integrity, thereby jeopardizing their access to real, enduring opportunities later on. Success without maintaining integrity and reliability is failure. Anyone can lie, cheat or steal, and maybe get away with it once, but it is no way to build an entrepreneurial career.

A recent study of 130 members of the Small Company Management Program at Harvard Business School confirmed how important this issue was in their businesses. Most simply said it was probably the single most important factor in their long-term successes. [4]

Decisiveness, Urgency and Patience. One of the paradoxes facing the entrepreneur is the simultaneous need for immediate decisiveness and urgency to get things done and achieve results, and the need for a longer term view and the patience to manage for the longer haul. The entrepreneur is at once a doer and a visionary. The vision of building a substantial enterprise that will contribute something lasting and relevant to the world, and realizing a capital gain, requires the patience to stick to the task for five to ten years or more.

Dealing with Failure. Using failure as a way of learning, to better understand the causes of the failure in order to avoid similar problems in the future, is another important feature of the entrepreneurial approach to things. There is an old saying that the cowboy never thrown from a horse hasn't ridden many! The iterative, trial-and-error nature of becoming a successful entrepreneur makes serious setbacks an integral part of the learning process.

The most effective entrepreneurs are realistic enough to expect such difficulties. Further, they do not become disappointed, discouraged, or depressed by a setback or failure. More typically they see in adversity and difficult times some opportunities as well, and see possible victory in situations where most people can only see defeat. They find promise where others find pessimism. They see opportunity where others mostly see obstacles.

4   J. A. Timmons and H. H. Stevenson, "Entrepreneurship Education in the 80's," Harvard Business School,1983.

Being intent on succeeding, entrepreneurs are not afraid of failing. People who fear failure will neutralize whatever achievement motivation they may possess. They will tend to engage in very easy tasks, where there is little chance of failure; or in very difficult (chance) situations, where they can not be held personally responsible if they don't succeed.

Team Builder and Hero Maker. Entrepreneurs who create and build substantial enterprises are not the lone-wolf, super independent types. They do not need to collect all the credit for the effort, nor feel the need to prove they did it "all by myself." Just the opposite characterizes their efforts. They recognize that it is rarely possible to build a substantial business working alone, and they actively build a team. They have the ability to make heroes out of the people they attract, by giving responsibility and sharing credit for accomplishments. In the corporate setting, this "hero-making" ability is identified as an essential attribute of successful entrepreneurial managers. [5]

These hero-makers, of both the independent and corporate varieties, share common attitudes and traits. They are determined to make the pie bigger and better for everyone, rather than jealously hoarding a tiny pie to themselves. They have a capacity for objective interpersonal relationships as well, which enables them to smooth out individual differences of opinion by keeping attention focused on the common goal to be achieved.

Can They Be Learned?

Which, and to what extent, can any of these and other entrepreneurial attitudes and actions be learned or acquired?

[5] D. L. Bradford and A. R. Cohen, *Managing For Excellence*, Wiley, 1984.

A consensus has emerged that, yes, you can definitely work on developing, practicing and refining them. Some will require more painstaking effort than others, and much will depend upon the motivation of the individual to grow. Developing an entrepreneurial mind-set isn't all that much different from learning in general: people have an astounding capacity to learn and change if they are motivated and committed to do so.

These entrepreneurial attributes are not just a summary of current academic research. They are the qualities that entrepreneurs themselves believe are in large part responsible for their success. Attendees at the Smaller Company Management Program at Harvard Business School were asked an open-ended question: What are the most critical concepts, skills and know-how for running your business—today and five years hence?

Their answers were very revealing: most mentioned mental attitudes and philosophies based on entrepreneurial attitudes rather than specific skills or organizational concepts! The answers are gathered together here as a sort of entrepreneur's creed.

FIGURE OUT HOW TO MAKE IT WORK.

ANYTHING IS POSSIBLE IF YOU BELIEVE YOU
    CAN DO IT.

THE CUP IS HALF-FULL, NOT HALF-EMPTY.

DO THINGS DIFFERENTLY.

MAKING MONEY IS MORE FUN THAN SPENDING IT.

TAKE PRIDE IN YOUR ACCOMPLISHMENTS:
    IT'S CONTAGIOUS.

DON'T WASTE TIME TRYING TO CUT SMALLER
    SLICES OF THE PIE: MAKE IT BIGGER.

The Non-Entrepreneurial Mind

There is also a non-entrepreneurial mind, whose assumptions and behaviors spell trouble for a new venture. These attitudes are observable in entrepreneurs who fail, or at least raise enough havoc so that the venture is at best among the "living dead." There is no research on this topic, other than broad-brush abstractions about "management as the leading cause of failure," but there are intriguing findings about "hazardous thought patterns" that may contribute to bad judgement among aircraft pilots—there are parallels between the piloting task and leading an emerging company. Some of these hazardous thought patterns among pilots have been observed as prevalent among entrepreneurs who fail:

Invulnerability. The attitude that nothing disastrous can happen. People with this notion are likely to take unnecessary chances and unwise risks. This behavior obviously would affect flying an airplane or launching a company.

Machismo. This describes people who try to prove they are better than others, who can beat others. They may try to prove themselves by taking large risks, and may try to impress others by exposing themselves to danger. This thought pattern goes beyond overconfidence. Foolish head-to-head competition and irrational take-over battles may be good business examples of this behavior.

Anti-authority. Some people resent control of their actions by any outside authority. Their approach is, "Don't tell me. No one can tell me what to do!" Contrast this thought pattern with the tendency of successful entrepreneurs to seek and use feedback in order to attain their goals and to improve their performance, and their propensity to seek team members and the necessary resources to execute their opportunity.

Impulsiveness. Facing a moment of decision, some people feel they must do something, do anything, and do it quickly. They fail to explore the implications of their actions, and do not review alternatives before acting.

Outer Control. This is the opposite of the internal locus of control characteristic of successful entrepreneurs. People with the trait of outer control feel they can do little, if anything, to control what happens to them. If things go well, they attribute it to good luck. If things go poorly they blame bad luck. [6]

In addition to these thought patterns are three others which have been observed by others:

Perfectionism. Perfectionism (not to be confused with high standards) is the enemy of the entrepreneur. The time and cost of attaining perfection invariably result in an opportunity window being slammed shut by a more decisive and nimble competitor, or disappearing altogether after a leap-frog in technology.

Know-It-All. Entrepreneurs who think they have all the answers usually have very few. To make matters worse, they often fail to recognize what they do not know. Good people and good opportunities find their way elsewhere.

6 Berl Brechner, "A Question of Judgement," *Flying*, May 1981, pp. 47-52.

Counter-Dependency. An extreme and severe case of independence can be a limiting mind-set for entrepreneurs. Determined to accomplish things all by themselves, without a particle of help from anyone, these entrepreneurs often end up accomplishing very little. But it is *all theirs* to claim.

Not just anyone and any random set of thought patterns or attitudes are conducive to launching and growing a venture with great potential. The task is simply too complex and demanding. Yet the smart and aware individuals who must be drawn to a venture for it to be a success do seem to partake—in many variations and combinations—from the entrepreneurial qualities described in this chapter.

On the other hand, there are certain thoughts and actions which can be fatal for would-be founders of a new venture. Some have been have identified. If you see any of them—or other signs of a non-entrepreneurial mind—stop and ask yourself: Would you want to work for people who think and act this way? Or have them as partners? Or invest in their businesses? Or work with them as a customer? Or depend on them to supply your critical components?

4

What Does It Take?

The Demands and Sacrifices of Entrepreneurship

It is not enough simply to possess an entrepreneurial mind-set. There are external demands that have important implications for the entrepreneurial task, and for the eventual success or failure of a venture.

Successful entrepreneurs may think and act in common with successful people in other careers, but it is their willingness to take on the demands and sacrifices of entrepreneuring that is their principal distinguishing feature.

These demands and sacrifices are called "external" because they are imposed upon every entrepreneur by the nature of the job. You must be able to adapt yourself to them; they are fixed and unforgiving, and are occasionally rewarding and punishing.

Some of these external demands are: a knowledge of the business environment in which you want to launch your venture, apprenticeship and experience, people and team building, and creativity. Here are four which are not examined as thoroughly elsewhere in this book.

Need for Total Commitment. The entrepreneur lives under constant pressure—first to survive, then to stay alive, and always to grow and withstand competitor's thrusts. Entrepreneurs must be prepared to "give all" to the building of the business, particularly in the early start-up years. This demand has important implications for marriage, raising a family, and community involvement. To do all of these well while attempting to launch a high-potential venture is not a realistic burden for most people. On the other hand, research on small-business owners, whose ventures are not in the 15-20% of all ventures that are growth-oriented, high-potential firms, shows there is room for accommodating family and community priorities. In fact, owners of small businesses are probably dominated as much by personal and family considerations as by the profitability of the business.

Stress: The Cost of Accommodation. Stress, the emotional and physiological reaction to external events or circumstances, can be both good and bad for entrepreneurs. In any case, it is inevitable—so the more you understand how you react to stress, the more effectively you can maximize high performance and minimize exhaustion and frustration.

Two recent surveys suggest that very high degrees of both satisfaction and stress characterize founders to a greater degree than managers, regardless of the success of their ventures. Stress was measured by such physiological symptoms as insomnia, indigestion, and chest pains. Though the founders seemed to accept these discomforts as part of the price, the authors remarked that enduring this unpleasantness was not a healthy long-run strategy. "The trade-off needs to be reckoned beyond the immediate situation. An effective strategy measures costs against benefits.... The price of corporate health should not be the loss of individual well-being."

Further, the authors attempted to correlate loneliness and stress, recognizing that "loneliness is significantly related to negative evaluations of physical self; greater loneliness is associated with tendencies to derogate health and appearance." The study did find a high degree of correlation between loneliness and stress, and, worse, found that the two states create a self-destructive cycle. The authors concluded with several practical ways to deal with the problem: first by recognizing its existence and then by controlling its determinants. [1]

Nonetheless, stress in the short run often produces extraordinary results, the type of action essential for entrepreneurs, especially in the start-up stage. Once this pattern of producing under pressure is established, it seems to get locked in; entrepreneurs tend to create new challenges to replace the ones they have met, and to continue to respond to them with a high level of effectiveness.

A point to consider in this regard: stopping stressful activity completely may be more harmful to your health than sticking with it while attempting to modify it. More than one CEO who has quit cold turkey suffered from months of malaise because he did not allow for a "cooling off" period, and one even suffered a heart attack. Like runners, entrepreneurs should probably follow a cooling-down regimen if they decide to decrease their level of activity.

Finally, to put the stress issue into perspective: to date there is no evidence that being an entrepreneur is any *more* stressful than certain other roles or careers. Doctors and nurses, senators, athletes, even teachers all face extraordinary workloads and the same stressful pressures and family trade-offs that high-growth entrepreneurs do. The personal price you must pay to realize your ambitions and achieve exceptional goals is high, regardless of career choice.

Economic and Professional Values. Business (unlike social or nonprofit) entrepreneurs must share the key values of the private enterprise system: private ownership, profits,

1 *Frontiers of Entrepreneurship Research,* 1982-1984.

capital gains, responsible growth. These dominant economic values need not necessarily exclude social or other values. But the realities of the competitive market economy seem to require a belief in or at least a tolerance of these values.

Personal values can have a profound effect on the development of the team and the business itself. An exception appears to be high-technology entrepreneurship. A study of high-technology entrepreneurs found that aesthetic and theoretical values were strongest. These values of entrepreneurs who spawned their ventures in the research labs of universities, government research centers, or medical laboratories seem to reflect the environments and backgrounds from which they came.

Ethics. Historically, the entrepreneur has tended to possess what is called "situational" ethics, defined by the needs and demands of the situation, rather than by some external, rigid code of conduct applied uniformly regardless of different conditions and circumstances. The need to examine your own ethical stance, and that of your partners and associates, is key to launching and growing a successful venture. Guarding carefully your reputation for integrity and ethical dealing is central to long-term success.

The Bottom Line

Despite all the demands, the stressful nature of being a lead entrepreneur, and the personal and family sacrifices involved, the bottom line is revealing. Increasing evidence about the careers and job satisfaction of entrepreneurs points to the same conclusion: if they had to do it over, not only would more become entrepreneurs again, but they would also do it earlier in their careers! They report higher personal satisfaction with their lives and their careers than their managerial counterparts.   Nearly three times as many entrepreneurs as managers say they plan never to retire. And living and working where and how they want to is a source of great satisfaction.

Financially, there is no doubt that successful growth-minded entrepreneurs enjoy higher incomes and net worths than career managers in large companies. In addition, their successful harvest of a company usually means a capital gain of several million dollars or more, and with it an entire new array of very attractive opportunities to do whatever they choose with the rest of their lives.

5

Interviewing an Entrepreneur

If entrepreneuring is new to you—you have not really known or worked with any entrepreneurs—then you will find it helpful to get to know at least one. Some questions and guidelines are given below for conducting an interview with a successful entrepreneur. A useful criterion is someone who has started a company within the past five years, which now exceeds $1 million in sales and is profitable. (Someone whose company is not profitable may give you some of the wrong lessons, or only rationalizations.)

The specific purpose for your interview with an entrepreneur is to gain information and insight about the entrepreneur's reasons, strategies, approaches and motivations for starting and owning a business, so as to help you sharpen your own ideas about who entrepreneur is and what he or she does. The more general purpose is to give you practice in using the interviewing process as a way to gather information and impressions about an unfamiliar topic.

You will learn more if you act more like an interested listener and less like a participant in "Twenty Questions." Jotting down direct quotes as evidence of motivations or reasons is more effective when you go back over your notes than statements such as "highly motivated individual." In other words, learn as many specifics as you can.

If you and the interviewee are *both* comfortable with using a small tape recorder, this can be of great help to you later. However, taping interviews often creates more trouble than it solves, so you will have to feel your way and follow your instincts on this matter.

Information-gathering through interviewing is a valuable skill for entrepreneurs to have, since they can learn a lot in a short time by talking to others. Your preparation should include the following steps:

- Define the purpose of the interview.
- Identify specific questions you would like to have answered, as well as general areas of information you would like to know more about. The combination of closed-end questions (How did you get the idea for your venture?) and open-ended ones (Could you tell me about...?) will help to keep the interview focused, yet will allow for unexpected comments and insights.
- Approach the person or persons you have selected and make an appointment to see them, at their convenience. Explain why you want to see them, and set a realistic estimate on how much time you will need.
- Be prepared to listen, as well as to ask.

After the interview has been completed, you have two more important steps to take:

- Write the interviewee a note to thank him or her for the time. This is more than a courtesy; it will also help the interviewee to remember you favorably if you want to contact that person again.

- Evaluate the interview. Write down the information in some form that will be helpful to you later on. Make a note of what you didn't find out, as well as what you did learn.

There is no one "right way" to structure an interview. The one suggested here has several merits, however. It is easy to use because it is chronological. And it has been tested successfully on many occasions.

It is suggested that you ask three open-ended questions, each of which assumes a number of closed-end questions, which you can ask directly if the entrepreneur does not supply the information as he is telling his story.

1. Would you tell me about yourself before you started your first venture?
- Did you have entrepreneurial parents, relatives or close friends?
- Who were your role models?
- What is your education/military experience? In hindsight, was it helpful?
- What was your previous work experience? Was it helpful?
- In particular, do you have sales or marketing experience? How important was it to starting your company?

2. How did you start your venture?
- How did you spot the opportunity?
- What were your goals?
- How did you evaluate the opportunity in terms of the critical elements for success? The competition? The market?
- Did you find or have partners? What kind of planning did you do? What kind of financing?

- Did you write a start-up business plan of any kind? Tell me about it.
- How much time did it take from the conception to the first day of business? How many hours a day did you spend working on it?
- How much capital did it take? How long did it take to reach a positive cash flow and breakeven sales volume? Tell me about the pressures and crises during that early survival period.
- What outside help did you get from experienced advisors? Lawyers? Accountants? Tax experts? Patent lawyers?
- What was your family situation at the time?
- What did you perceive to be your own strengths? Weaknesses?
- What did you perceive to be the strengths of your venture? Weaknesses?

3. Once you got going, what happened then?
- What were the most difficult gaps to fill and problems to solve as you began to grow rapidly?
- When you looked for key people as partners, advisors or managers, were there any personal attributes or attitudes you were especially seeking because you knew they would fit with you, and were important to success? Were (or are) there any attributes among partners and advisors that you would definitely try to avoid?
- Have things become more predictable?
- Do you spend more, the same or less time with your business now than in the early years?
- Do you now feel more managerial and less entrepreneurial?
- In terms of the future, do you plan to harvest? To maintain? To expand?

- When do you plan to retire?
- Have you met your goals? Have they changed?
- Has your family situation changed?

In conclusion, here are some questions which some entre-preneurs enjoy talking about:

- What do you consider your most valuable asset—the thing that enabled you to "make it?"
- If you had it to do over again, would you? In the same way? Would you do anything differently?
- Looking back, what do you feel are the most critical concepts, skills, attitudes and know-how you needed to get your company started and grown to where it is today? What about five years from now? To what extent can any of these be learned?
- Some people say there is a lot of stress being an entrepreneur. What have you experienced? How would you say it compares with other "hot seat" jobs, such as the head of a big company, or a partner in a large law, consult-ing or accounting firm?
- What are the things you find personally rewarding and satisfying as an entrepreneur? What have been the rewards, risks and trade-offs?
- Who should try to be an entrepreneur? Can you give me any ideas there?
- What advice would you give an aspiring entrepreneur?

6

The Entrepreneurial Manager

As a venture accelerates and grows, the key to sustaining growth, and realizing eventual harvest, is developing competencies to manage that growth. Evidence suggests that most new ventures that flourish beyond survival are headed by an entrepreneur who is also an effective entrepreneurial manager. For instance, an INC. magazine survey of the heads of the top 100 ventures showed that the majority of their founders were still the CEOs several years later when they had attained sales of $10 million, $25 million, even $50 million or more.

These and other data seem to defy previous notions that entrepreneurs can start but cannot manage fast-growing, innovative companies. The truth is probably somewhere in between. But one thing is apparent: The competencies and skills required for a vibrant, growing, entrepreneurial company cannot be primarily administrative efficiency, emphasis on maintenance, resource ownership and institutional formalization. To grow a new venture that continues to innovate and exert a competitive edge calls for the managerial skills to cope effectively with a high level of change, chaos and uncertainty.[1]

---

1 For another useful view of the stages of development of a firm and the required management capabilities, see Carroll V. Kroeger, "Management Development and the Small Firm," *California Management Review*, vol. 17, no. 1 (Fall 1974), pp. 41-47.

Consider what the following situations have in common, the pressures and demands they foster, and what it takes to manage each one effectively:

• The president of a rapidly growing small computer company sums up what it's like to develop and market new products: "In our business it takes 6–12 months to develop a new computer, ready to bring to the market. Product technology obsolescence is running about 9–12 months."

• The head of Litton's microwave oven division notes a critical requirement: "In 1981 our sales were $13 million and we had 275 employees. Our long-range plan called for building our sales volume to $100 million in five to seven years (40% a year compounded). Having studied the market for the previous two years I was convinced that the only limit on our growth was our organization's inability to grow as rapidly as the market opportunities." [2]

• A middle manager in yet another mushrooming firm finds the pace hectic, with lots of uncertainties and ambiguities: "If you like to know exactly where things are, who's doing what, and when; prefer a structured situation; and need to know exactly where things stand—then you'll go nuts working here."

• A manufacturing VP comments on his best managers: "They are jugglers that keep all this glued together: they have a knack for blending and balancing the competing, and often conflicting, demands, and for creatively solving problems. They aren't distracted by the chaos and confusion—they thrive on it."

• Apollo Computer, the highly successful Massachusetts firm, grew from its inception in 1981 to 5,000 employees in five years. One new manager in the firm told what the turbu-

2 W. W. George, "Task Teams for Rapid Growth," *Harvard Business Review*, March-April, 1977.

lence was like: "We had no organization charts or name plates on the doors. We were growing so rapidly that all that would have been obsolete by the time it was printed up. A lot of us didn't even have regular job titles, since they were in constant flux as well."

Managing and growing a new venture is obviously a different managerial game than working in a large, older, stable company. Change seems to be constant, high levels of ambiguity and uncertainty are a way of life, and both compound rapidly, often leading to instability. The constancy of change pilfers the already precious commodity of time. Time is compressed by the shorter leads, lags and life cycles of technology, product development, manufacturing and marketing. The organization must absorb growth and assimilate change while attaining cohesion as well as financial and operating control. One net effect of all this is a series of compounding shock waves rolling through the venture by way of new customers, new technologies, new competitors, new markets, and new people.

For managers to excel under these conditions requires a resiliency and responsiveness that is uncommon. Without it, the shock waves can lead to instability and crises before the real numbers detect it. And it's not difficult to envision the industries where such requirements are commonplace: electronics and aerospace in the 1960s, small computers, integrated circuits and silicon chips in the 1970s, and telecommunications and microcomputers in the 1980s, to note a few.

There seems to be an entrepreneurial creativity in these firms from the outset. But it is a kind of creativity tempered by a keen eye on the marketplace and the goal of commercialization. Technological elegance for its own sake may have far less to do with longer term success than is commonly believed. Unless market share is protected by the monopoly of a patent, a technological lead alone may not be critical.

In the late 1960s and early 1970s as many as seventy new firms were launched to exploit the new technology in small-scale computing. Many industry experts acknowledge that among the dominant industry leaders today, such as Digital Equipment, Data General, Control Data and Prime Computer, some other firms started at the same time actually had more elegant technology in their products. Yet most of them lacked the entrepreneurial savvy and ingenuity needed to survive.

Television did not come about by a succession of improvements in radio. The jet plane did not emerge from those engineers and scientists attempting to develop a better and better piston engine plane. If this pattern holds for future technology the implications are clear: we would not expect the major breakthroughs in energy to come from the oil companies, nor in electrically powered vehicles from the automotive industry. Rather, more innovative and entrepreneurial smaller, rapid growth firms will be the major source of innovations.

One of the differences in managing the entrepreneurial venture is the non-linear and non-parametric event. Many events don't follow straight lines nor progress arithmetically; rather, they occur in bunches, in step-wise leaps. For instance, a sales force doubles in a year and a half rather than eight years. Manufacturing capacity is tripled in two years with two new plants rather than increased overtime, followed by a third shift nine months later, and maybe a new plant three years hence. In short, the increments are lurches rather than smooth and digestible steps.

Yet another characteristic of managing such a venture is a counter-intuitive, unconventional pattern of decision-making. What approach, for example, should be taken by one company to developing and introducing three new computers in an uncertain, risky marketplace? [3] Each proposed new computer appears to be going after the same end-user market, and each project head is similarly enthusiastic, confident and determined about succeeding.

Conventional wisdom suggests that the company should (a) determine the size and growth rates of each market segment, (b) estimate the future revenues, costs and capital requirements, (c) compare the discounted, present-value cashflow streams, and (d) select the project with the highest combined yield.

This is a fundamentally sound, useful decision-making process—*when one best alternative exists* (and assuming that accurate and relevant information is obtainable when needed, at a reasonable cost in dollars and management time—luxuries rarely occurring in most entrepreneurial situations).

What may be overlooked is that most rapidly growing companies have *many* excellent alternatives. High-margin opportunities outstrip resources. And more commonly, the newness of technology, immaturity of the marketplace, and rapid discovery of further applications makes it virtually impossible to know which of any three product proposals is best.

What did this computer firm do? They supported all three new products at once. And what did they learn? A significant new business was built around each one, with new market niches being discovered simultaneously.

3 Tracy Kidder, *The Soul of a New Machine*, 1981.

Further, it confirmed their belief that under tumultuous conditions of rapidly changing technology and markets, unconventional approaches can pay off. There is simply not the time, certainty nor mature information available to provide the proof expected in more stable circumstances.

Many entrepreneurial ventures also defy conventional organizational patterns and structures. It is not uncommon to find a firm that has grown to $150 million or more in annual sales and still have no formal organizational chart. If one does exist it is inevitably out of date. It changes frequently—one firm had eight major reorganizations in its first five years. It is flat, with few management layers, and with easy access to the top decision-makers. It is a fluid structure, not one rigidly defined by policy manuals, detailed procedures, or other early signs of bureaucratic sclerosis. More often than not, the process and organization encourages people to wander around and talk to who they need to see in order to get things done—now.

There is an informality to the organization as well. But its fluidity and informality do not mean casualness or sloppiness when it comes to goals, standards, or clarity of direction and purpose. Rather it translates into flexible and effective response to rapid change, while maintaining financial and operational cohesion. These firms don't confuse informality with a lack of discipline.

Managing growth and innovation involves some managerial tasks and roles not found in most mature and stable environments. For one thing, the classical divisions of responsibility and authority are counterproductive in a quickly growing venture. There it's quite different: do what is needed to get the job done, attain the goal, or meet the deadline. Results usually require close collaboration with people other than those reporting directly. Effective managers need to be especially skillful at managing conflict, resolving differences, balancing multiple viewpoints and demands, and building teamwork and consensus. These skills are particularly difficult when working with others outside an immediate "chain of formal command."

Given these special requirements, what do the effective managers do differently? They focus on goals, the market and customers, rather than on whose territory or whose prerogatives are being challenged. Such managers appear quite unconcerned about status, power and personal control. They are more concerned about making sure tasks, goals and roles are clear than whether the organization chart is current, or whether their offices and furnishings reflect their current status. Likewise, they are more concerned about the strength of arguments affecting a decision than the title or position of the individual doing the arguing.

This value system also expresses a different view of status: it is earned by accomplishments, and cemented in the promise of future achievements. Elegant office space, special privileges and titles aren't the vogue. Contrast this with a multi-billion-pound but stagnant firm in England. There are reportedly no less than 29 different makes and models of automobiles used in the firm to signify position, from Rolls-Royce through Morris Mini.

In summary, there appears to be a breed of hybrid managers in innovative and growing entrepreneurial companies who fit neither the stereotype of founding entrepreneurs nor the middle manager in a large, established company. The particularly effective ones do things differently. They have some unique skills, especially critical in managing rapidly growing companies and which are quite useful elsewhere as well. The skills have a great deal to do with the way these managers exert influence over others. But the skills also describe many of the demands and tasks that appear so frequently in innovative and growing firms.

Creating Clarity Out of Confusion. Entrepreneurial managers have a knack for forging clarity out of the chaos, ambiguity and constant change they face. The managers who work with them perceive that entrepreneurial managers are able adroitly to define and gain agreement on who has what responsibility and authority, and who does what with and to whom. Further, they do this in a way that builds motivation and commitment to cross-departmental and corporate goals, not just to parochial interests.

But this is not perceived by other managers as an effort to jealously carve out and guard personal turf and prerogatives. Rather, it is seen as a genuine effort to clarify roles, tasks, and responsibilities, and to make sure there is accountability and appropriate approvals. This doesn't work unless the manager is seen as willing to relinquish his priorities and power in the interest of an overall goal. It also requires skill in making sure the appropriate people are included in setting cross-functional or cross-departmental goals, and in making decisions. And when this doesn't go as smoothly as hoped, the most effective managers work through to an agreement, rather than dash to a shared superior to break the tie.

Managers new to an entrepreneurial company, and accustomed to a traditional chain of command where "end arounds" and "two-uppers" and "two-downers" are taboo, are often baffled and frustrated in their new role. While some may be quite effective in dealing with their own subordinates, it is an entirely new task to manage and work with peers, other's subordinates, and even superiors outside their chain of command. Getting results from people over whom you have no direct authority requires special skill.

Solving Conflicts and Sharing Power. The most effect-ive managers are more creative and skillful in handling conflicts, generating consensus decisions, and sharing their power and information. They are able to get people to open up, instead of clamming up. They get problems out on the table instead of under the rug, and they don't become defensive when others disagree with their views. They seem to know that high-quality decisions require a rapid flow of information in all directions, and that knowledge, competence, logic and evidence should prevail over official status or formal rank in the organization.

The way they manage and resolve conflicts is intriguing. For one thing, they are able to get potential adversaries to be creative and collaborative in making the pie bigger in the interest of an overall organizational goal. They do this by seeking a reconciliation of viewpoints, rather than emphasiz-ing differences, and by blending ideas, rather than playing the role of hard-nose negotiator or devil's advocate to force a pet solution.

They are willing to risk personal vulnerability in this process—often by giving up their own power and resources. Perhaps they can do this because they have a clear under-standing of the longer term consequences if they don't: a win-lose, adversarial climate; zero-some games; less creative problem solving; and a power and control-oriented organiza-tion that eventually collapses of its own weight and myopia over managerial prerogatives.

The trade-offs aren't easy: at the outset such an approach involves more managers, takes more time, and often appears to yield few immediate results. Up front it seems like a more painful way to manage.

Later on, however, the gains from the motivation, commitment and teamwork which are anchored in a consensus are striking. For one thing, there is swiftness and decisiveness in actions and follow through, since the negotiating, compromising, and accepting of priorities is history. For another, new disagreements that emerge generally don't bring progress to a halt, since there is both high clarity and broad acceptance of the overall goal and underlying priorities.

Encouraging Innovation and Calculated Risk-taking. Another form of entrepreneurial influence more effective managers use also has to do with creativity and innovativeness. Simply stated, they build confidence by encouraging innovation and calculated risk-taking, rather than by punishing or criticizing whatever is less than perfect. For another thing, they breed independent, entrepreneurial thinking by expecting and encouraging others to find and correct their own errors, and to solve their own problems.

This does not mean they follow a "throw them to the wolves" approach. Rather, they are perceived by their peers and other managers as accessible, and willing to help when needed. When it is appropriate, they go to bat for their peers and subordinates, even when they know they can't always win. And they provide the necessary resources to enable others to do the job.

Building Trust. The most effective managers are perceived as trustworthy; they behave in ways that create trust. How do they do this? They are straightforward; they do what they say they are going to do. They are not rumor carriers, nor purveyors of gossip. They are open and spontaneous, rather than guarded and cautious. They are perceived as being honest and direct.

They get results because they understand that the task of managing in a rapidly growing company usually goes well beyond chain of command. They become known as the creative problem solvers who have a knack for blending and balancing multiple views and demands. Their calculated risk-taking works out more often than it fails. And they have a reputation for developing human capital—they groom other effective growth managers by example and mentoring.

Launching a new venture and making it succeed depends upon a lot of factors. One enormous difficulty is to know what really works and what really counts. There are certain critical competencies and skills which successful entrepreneurs believe are vital. You will undoubtedly need others to go very far, but without these minimums the lifeline of the enterprise is short, and the ink is red.

7

Intrapreneurial Management

One significant consequence of the new wave of entrepreneurship in America is a heightened awareness of its benefits for large companies. Never before has there been more attention paid to the need for entrepreneurship *within* large organizations. What have researchers and writers concluded about how the best-run established companies are managed? Surprise, surprise: they have top and middle managers with a flair for entrepreneurial management! They encourage and practice many of the entrepreneurial approaches discussed here.

R. M. Kanter argues that American corporations will prosper only to the extent they understand, initiate and carry out innovational changes at every level of the organization. She identifies three sets of skills as necessary for entrepreneurial change-agents which can produce integrative, innovation-stimulating environments: power and persuasion skills; the ability to manage the greater problems accompanying team and employee participation; and an understanding of how change is designed and constructed in an organization. [1]

While being a corporate entrepreneur necessitates buying into an already existing value system and organizational culture that has been created by others, many of the practices and competencies are the same. Kanter sums it up this way:

---

1 R. M. Kanter, *The Change Masters*, 1983.

"In short, individuals do not have to be doing 'big things' in order to have their cumulative accomplishments eventually result in big performance for the company... . They are only rarely the inventors of the 'breakthrough' system. They are only rarely doing something that is totally unique or that no one, in any organization, ever thought of before. Instead, they are often applying ideas that have proved themselves elsewhere, or they are rearranging parts to create a better result, or they are noting a potential problem before it turns into a catastrophe and mobilizing the actions to anticipate and solve it."

What does this mean for middle managers within large organizations? What do entrepreneurial and innovative middle managers do, and how do their organizations treat them? For one thing, they are comfortable with change, and see unmet needs as opportunities. Further, they have clarity of direction, carefully select projects, possess long time horizons, and see setbacks as temporary. They are known for thorough preparation, and operate with a team-oriented, participative management style. Finally, they practice perseverance, persistence and discretion. [2]

Sound familiar? It should not come as a surprise. After all, what works, works—size of organization is no barrier.

Most entrepreneurial businesses enjoy substantial gross margins, often 30, 50 even 60 percent or more. This certainly provides a marvelous cushion for mistakes and errors, and some breathing space as new people learn new jobs in new technologies and markets. But if price competition suddenly appears, margins erode and the safety cushion with it. The organization may come unraveled at this point, if top management has failed to develop entrepreneurial middle

_____

[2] R. M. Kanter, "Middle Manager As Innovator," *Harvard Business Review*, July-August, 1982.

management. Linking a plan to create human capital at the middle management and supervisory levels with the overall business strategy is thus an essential first step.

How does one get middle managers to pursue and practice entrepreneurial excellence? Once again, some of the important fundamentals practiced by team-builder entrepreneurs—who are more intent on getting results than just getting their own way—may be emulated. We can distinguish between the "heroic manager" whose need to be in control in many instances actually may stifle cooperation, and the "post-heroic manager," a developer who actually brings about excellence in modern organizations. [3]

A good example of leading initiatives to foster an entrepreneurial culture is underway at Pepsi Cola Corporation, North America. Its new president, Roger Enrico, is doing more than just talking or writing about it. As new CEO of Pepsi, one of his early initiatives was to develop a strategy and culture to encourage entrepreneurial managers. He summarized six critical factors:

Understand the market: know the business you are in and stay in that business.

Set high performance standards: by starting with yourself; develop short-run objectives without sacrificing long-run results.

Provide responsive, personal leadership: you don't manage through memos and computer printouts, you do it eyeball to eyeball, and by energizing ideas.

Encourage individual initiative.

Help others to succeed.

Develop your own network for success.

Above all, maintain commitment and integrity.

---

3 D. Bradford and A. Cohen, *Managing for Excellence*, 1984.

The convergence of these independent viewpoints with the earlier discussion on the lead entrepreneur is far more than coincidental. The message is too powerful to ignore: As long as the opportunity is there, and has been spotted, entrepreneurial management actions can convert opportunity into results. These principles are more important than the size of the organization, it stage of growth, the education of the entrepreneurial manager, or any combination.

8

What Skills are Needed?

After you have absorbed the key messages about the entrepreneurial manager—especially the sometimes conflicting,
sometimes overlapping characteristics of the entrepreneurial
domain and the managerial domain—it might be useful for
you to assess your own management competencies and those
of your team. If you consider yourself to be highly "entrepreneurial," do you or your team members have the management skills needed to deal with a growing venture? On the
other hand, if you consider yourself to be a competent manager joining an entrepreneurial team, will you be able to
adapt to the different climate of that group?

The inventory in this chapter is a comprehensive list of
management competencies. Its seven major dimensions include four key areas of functional skills—marketing, finance,
production and operations, and microcomputer skills—and
three areas of cross-functional skills—administration, interpersonal and team work, and law and taxation.

As you go through the list, there are important points
you should keep in mind. One of the greatest strengths of
successful entrepreneurs is that they *know what they do and
don't know.* They have a disciplined, intellectual honesty
about this which prevents their optimism from becoming
myopic delusion, and their dreams from becoming blind
ambition.

Being able to size up your own strengths and weaknesses in this manner is an important ability to cultivate. The management competency inventory which follows can be a useful tool in identifying the skills you have and those you need to develop.

• The assumption behind this exercise is that a systematic recording and analysis of your experiences and skills can (a) help you see where you have been, (b) help you pinpoint what you do and don't know, and (c) provide some direction for using what you have learned about yourself to benefit your venture.

• Clearly, a complex set of factors goes into making someone a successful entrepreneur. No individual has all of the managerial skills or personal qualities defined in the exercises. The presence or absence of any single dimension does not guarantee success or failure as an entrepreneur. Knowing that you do *not* have a certain skill—and knowing where to get it—is clearly as valuable as knowing you already do have it. And remember, there is no substitute for a good opportunity which has gross margins of 60% or more!

You will note that a space has been left at the end of each major skill section (e.g., "Marketing") for you to sum the number of checks in each of the three columns. Comparison of the number of checks in the "know well," "limited knowledge," and "unfamiliar" columns of each major section should provide a useful way of measuring your overall level of competence in that area.

If you feel you have no basis whatsoever for a self-evaluation, you may simply leave a blank, although the (c) choice would also be appropriate. Some technical skills (engineering, designing, etc.) unique to your venture may not be included. Simply add any of these areas to the list and evaluate them for yourself.

The important thing is to identify the critical skills required for your venture to succeed—the ones without which you will fail. Then, by focusing on which ones you know and don't know—but need to have—you can figure out what to do about it.

Management Competency Inventory

For each competency, place a check in the column that best describes your degree of experience and accomplishment in that area:

  a) you know well and have proven results doing it.
  b) you have limited knowledge, need backup.
  c) you are unfamiliar, have no proven results.

Marketing Skills

Market Research and Evaluation: Able to find and interpret industry and competitor information; to design and conduct customer and market research studies, and analyze and interpret study results; are familiar with questionnaire design and sampling techniques.

                                   ___ a ___ b ___ c

New Product Planning: Experience in new-product introductions, including marketing testing, prototype testing, and development of price/sales/merchandising and distribution plans for new products.

                                   ___ a ___ b ___ c

Product Management: Able to integrate market information, perceived needs, R&D and advertising into a rational product plan; able to understand market penetration and breakeven.

                                   ___ a ___ b ___ c

Product Pricing: Able to determine competitive pricing and margin structures, and to position products in terms of price; able to develop pricing policies that maximize profits.

___ a ___ b ___ c

Marketing Planning: Experienced in planning overall sales, advertising, and promotion programs and in deciding on and setting up effective distributor or sales representation systems.

___ a ___ b ___ c

Sales Management: Able to organize, supervise, and motivate a direct sales force; able to analyze territory and account sales potential and to manage a sales force to obtain maximum share of market.

___ a ___ b ___ c

Direct Selling: Experience in identifying, meeting, and developing new customers; demonstrated success in closing a sale.

___ a ___ b ___ c

Distribution Management: Able to organize and manage the flow of product from manufacturing through distribution channels to ultimate customer; includes familiarity with shipping costs, scheduling techniques, carriers, etc.

___ a ___ b ___ c

Service: Able to perceive service needs of particular products; experience in determining service and spare part requirements, handling customer complaints, and managing a service organization.

___ a ___ b ___ c

Marketing Totals   ___ a ___ b ___ c

Operations/Technical Skills

Manufacturing Management: Know the production process; know machines, manpower and space required; experience in managing production within time, cost, and quality constraints.

___ a ___ b ___ c

Inventory Control: Familiar with techniques of controlling materials flow for in-process and finished-goods inventory.

___ a ___ b ___ c

Cost Analysis and Control: Able to calculate labor and materials costs, develop standard cost system, conduct variance analyses, calculate overtime labor needs, and control costs.

___ a ___ b ___ c

Quality Control: Able to set up inspection systems and standards for effective quality control of incoming, in-process, and finished materials.

___ a ___ b ___ c

Production Scheduling and Flow: Able to analyze work flow, plan and manage production process; manage work flow; able to calculate schedules and flows for rising sales levels.

___ a ___ b ___ c

Purchasing: Able to identify appropriate sources of supply, negotiate supplier contracts, and manage incoming flow of material into inventory; familiar with economic order quantities and discount advantages.

___ a ___ b ___ c

Job Evaluation: Able to analyze worker productivity and need for additional help; able to calculate cost-saving aspects of temporary versus permanent help.

___ a ___ b ___ c

Operations/Technical Skills Totals ___ a ___ b ___ c

Financial Skills

Raising Capital: Able to decide how best to acquire funds for start-up and growth; able to forecast funds needs, prepare budgets; familiar with sources and vehicles of short and long-term formal and informal financing.

___ a ___ b ___ c

Cash Flow Management: Able to project cash requirements, set up cash controls and manage the firm's cash position; identify how much capital is needed, when, and when you will run out of cash.

___ a ___ b ___ c

Credit and Collection Management: Able to develop credit policies and screening criteria; can age receivables and payables; understand use of collection agencies; know when to start legal action.

___ a ___ b ___ c

Short-term Financing Alternatives: Understand payables management, use of interim financing such as bank loans, factoring of receivables, pledging and selling notes and contracts, bills of lading, bank acceptance; familiar with financial statements; budgeting and profit planning.

                                              ___ a ___ b ___ c

Familiar with Public and Private Offerings: Able to develop a business plan and offering memo that can be used to raise capital. Familiar with legal requirements of public and private stock offerings.

                                              ___ a ___ b ___ c

Bookkeeping and Accounting: Able to determine appropriate bookkeeping and accounting system as company starts and grows, including various ledgers and accounts.

                                              ___ a ___ b ___ c

Specific Skills: Cash flow analysis, breakeven analysis, contribution analysis, profit and loss, balance sheet.

                                              ___ a ___ b ___ c

                         Financial Skills Totals   ___ a ___ b ___ c

Microcomputer Skills

Spread Sheet Analysis

                                              ___ a ___ b ___ c

Word Processing

                                              ___ a ___ b ___ c

Database Access and Electronic Mail

                                              ___ a ___ b ___ c

Graphics   ___ a ___ b ___ c

                Microcomputer Skills Totals   ___ a ___ b ___ c

Administrative Skills

Problem Solving: Able to anticipate potential problems and to plan to avoid them; able to gather facts about problems, analyze them for *real* causes, and plan effective action to solve them; very thorough in dealing with details of particular problems and in following through.

                                                               ___ a ___ b ___ c

Communication: Able to communicate effectively and clearly—speaking and writing—to media, public, customers, peers, and subordinates.

                                                               ___ a ___ b ___ c

Planning: Able to set realistic and attainable goals, identify obstacles and develop detailed action plans to achieve goals; schedule own time very systematically.

                                                               ___ a ___ b ___ c

Decision Making: Able to make decisions on best analysis of incomplete data.

                                                               ___ a ___ b ___ c

Project Management: Skilled in organizing project teams, setting project goals, defining project tasks, and monitoring task completion in the face of problems and cost/quality constraints.

                                                               ___ a ___ b ___ c

Negotiating: Able to work effectively in a negotiating situation; able to balance quickly value given and value received.

___ a ___ b ___ c

Managing Outside Professionals: Able to identify, manage and guide appropriate legal, financial, banking, accounting, consulting and other necessary outside advisors.

___ a ___ b ___ c

Personnel Administration: Able to set up payroll, hiring, compensation, and training functions.

___ a ___ b ___ c

Administrative Skills Totals ___ a ___ b ___ c

Interpersonal and Team Skills

Leadership and Influence: Able to understand the relationships between tasks, the leader and the followers; able to lead in those situations where it is appropriate; willing to actively manage, supervise and control activities of others through directions, suggestions, etc.

___ a ___ b ___ c

Listening and Trust Building: Able to listen to and understand without interrupting or mentally preparing own rebuttal at the expense of hearing the message.

___ a ___ b ___ c

Helping: Able to ask for and provide help and to determine situations where assistance is warranted.

___ a ___ b ___ c

Feedback: Able to provide performance and interpersonal feedback to others that they find useful; able to receive feedback from others without becoming defensive or argumentative.

___ a ___ b ___ c

Conflict Management: Able to confront differences openly and to deal with them until resolution is obtained. Able to use evidence and logic. Share power.

___ a ___ b ___ c

Teamwork: Able to work well with others in pursuing common goals, especially when without formal power.

___ a ___ b ___ c

Developing Subordinates: Able to delegate responsibility and to coach subordinates in the development of their managerial capabilities.

___ a ___ b ___ c

Climate and Culture Building: Able to create, by the way you manage, a climate and spirit conducive to high performance; including ability to press for performance while rewarding work well done. Able to encourage innovation, initiative and calculated risk taking.

___ a ___ b ___ c

Interpersonal /Team Skills Totals ___ a ___ b ___ c

Knowledge of Applicable Law

Corporate and Securities Law: Familiar with the legalities of stock issues, incorporation, distribution agreements, leases, etc.

___ a ___ b ___ c

Contract Law: Familiar with contract procedures and requirements (government and commercial), including default, warranty, incentive provisions, fee structures, overhead, G & A allowable, etc.

___ a ___ b ___ c

Patent and Proprietary Rights Laws: Experienced with preparation and revision of patent applications; able to recognize a strong patent; familiar with claim requirements and proprietary rights.

___ a ___ b ___ c

Tax Law: Familiar with state and federal reporting requirements; Subchapter S, employee benefit and retirement plans, tax shelters, estate planning, fringe benefits, etc.

___ a ___ b ___ c

Real Estate Law: Familiar with leases, purchase offers, purchase and sale agreements, etc.

___ a ___ b ___ c

Investment Agreement Law: Familiar with issues relating to term sheets, investment agreements, employment and non-competition agreements, vesting, restricted stock agreements, etc.

___ a ___ b ___ c

Knowledge of Applicable Law Totals ___ a ___ b ___ c

Summary Questions

Which skills are "musts" for your venture?

Which of your management skills were highlighted as particularly strong?

Which ones were highlighted as particularly weak?

In what ways has your assessment of your management skills and entrepreneurial mind-set changed as a result of this exercise?

How can you compensate for and overcome the shortcomings you identified? Do you need one or more partners? When?

What areas do you need to explore further?

In terms of your career and venture, what management know-how or experience do you need to acquire?

What outside advisors can fill these gaps—legal, financial, technical, accounting, directors—and how can you find them?

9

Forming the
New Venture Team

Do you need a team to help you start up a new company? You should know that more fast-growing ventures are founded by teams than by individuals. There are successes founded by one person, but teams build substantial companies: lone founders are much less likely to build multi-million-dollar plus ventures. A venture also does not have to start with a full team, all taking the plunge into the business simultaneously. It may take some time for the team to come together as the firm grows.

Of course, not every solo venture is destined for the business boneyard. Many entrepreneurs seem to prefer the solo venture, or may have acquired a distaste for partners. You may not wish to become a team player. In that case, a team-founded venture is not for you.

Some lead entrepreneurs can be happy only if they are in complete control: they want employees, not partners. Others simply do not want to give up control to outside investors, or anyone else.

Take, for instance, an entrepreneur we shall call Ed. He founded a high-technology firm ten years ago that has grown steadily, but slowly, to nearly $2 million in sales. Recently, new patents and technological advances in his field drew interest from venture capitalists. But Ed turned down more than one offer for up to $5 million of *funding because the investors wanted to own 51% or more of his venture. He simply said, "I do not want to give up control of what I have worked so long and hard to create."*

Analyzing the Business

Analyzing the potential venture is a critical early need. This starts with the opportunity: a good one is one with durable profit potential that you can pursue—even if you currently do not control the resources to seize it. Given the opportunity you want to pursue, the question, "What business are we in?" is a fundamental but often neglected one. Every industry has ingredients that are critical to success, "absolute musts" if you are to compete at all. Identifying what appears to be the critical success variables in the industry has significant implications for team selection and the ultimate success of the venture.

What are the most important goals for the first two to three years of the business? They may be both financial and nonfinancial. Are these goals articulated in a specific, measurable, time-phased, and realistic manner? For example, have you prepared a monthly cash flow projection for the first year of your business?

What are the key tasks and activities needed to accomplish the goals? Clearly, many areas will be difficult to specify, but more detail is better than less.

Ventures usually prosper because they provide a unique product or service or because they secure a market niche. What things will make the venture distinct from its competition? What value and benefits can you add for your customers?

Relating effectively to the external environment—the technologies, markets, banks, institutions—is required for survival and growth. What are the critical external relationships for the venture, such as with lawyers, bankers, customers, suppliers, regulatory agencies?

Although there will be few precise answers to each question during early gestation of the venture, best estimates must be developed. Answers to these questions provide important background information for analyzing the needs for an entrepreneurial team.

Self-Assessment

If you are the founder, it is critical to the success of the venture that you understand *how* you decided to become an entrepreneur and *why* you chose the particular business. Self-assessment is therefore an essential early task. You must ask yourself: What do I want from my business? What are my expectations and aspirations? What life style and values are especially important to me? What are my family's expectations? What sacrifices are we prepared to make? Do we know what we are getting into?

What are my goals? What is the nature of my commitment? What kind of a risk-taker am I? How do I deal with failure? What are my motivations? How do I utilize feedback and seek needed help? What is required of the entrepreneur's job? What does the entrepreneur have to put up with? What are the resources I need to control?

What is my track record, my strengths and weaknesses? What things do I do extremely well—negotiating, marketing, finance, technical know-how, or people management? What do I need to learn? How do others size me up in terms of maturity?

What interpersonal skills do I have? How do I deal with and resolve differences? How do I feel about teamwork? How do others react to me as a team leader? Are there special demands unique to my venture and industry? Who will do what tasks?

The person in charge needs to know the business thoroughly and be committed to the venture's success. Successful entrepreneurs build on their strengths and former experience. In a start-up situation, the entrepreneur usually wears many hats. The more he or she can personally manage, the better.

As stressed in the previous chapter, knowing what you do and do not know is a key entrepreneurial perspective. Some important team issues follow from this. What skills and capabilities does the venture need beyond those the founder brings to the venture? If the founder cannot provide the needed capabilities, or cannot learn them in time, then someone on the venture team must have them. Whether the founder's personal strengths are of a technical or managerial nature, the focus is on daily operations or long-term development, other team members must fill the voids. Who are the people with the know-how and contacts I need in order to succeed? Often, these contacts will be with outside professionals and experts who are vital to the success of the venture. [1]

Forming a Team

There seem to be a multitude of ways in which venture partners come together. Some teams form by accidents of geography and common interest, others by virtue of past friendships. Other teams form simply because the members want to start a business, while others have an idea they feel responds to a market need.

1 For a useful discussion of finding and managing outsiders, see H. H. Stevenson and W. Sahlman, "How Small Companies Should Handle Advisors," *Harvard Business Review*, March-April 1988, pp 28-34.

Few teams seem to have exactly the same gestation process. Yet two distinct patterns are identifiable. First, one person has an idea for starting a business. Then one to four associates join as the venture takes form. Second, an entire team, or partnership, forms from the outset based on a shared idea, friendship, experience, or a host of other related factors. These two patterns are the principal "natural" processes of team formation.

What becomes of such naturally formed teams? About 95 percent of them seeking venture capital never get off the ground. They usually exhaust their own resources, and their commitment, before raising the capital necessary to launch the venture.

Of those that are funded, about one in twenty will become successful in three to five years. (Success to the investor roughly means a return in excess of five times the original investment in realizable capital gains.) Clearly, the odds against a highly successful venture are high. Even if the venture survives, the turnover among team members during the early years probably exceeds the national divorce rate.

These odds against success seem to be largely a result of the "natural" team formation and development just described. Ironically, a substantial amount of thought usually accompanies the decision of people to go into business together. Yet too much of the thinking focuses on such issues as titles, corporate name, letterhead, what kind of lawyer or accountant is needed, rather than, "Is this a good opportunity, do we know how to do the work, and will we do it?"

Fortunately for aspiring entrepreneurs, several fundamental issues can be considered systematically to make team formation and development a more organized, carefully thought-out process. This process can assist the new venture team to identify its staffing needs in a methodical way and to do a significantly better job of anticipating and dealing with the inevitable crises and conflicts that arise in the early stages of a new business.

Here is one example of an entrepreneurial team who took advantage of the planned approach:

Three technical men formed a company to manufacture gold-plating equipment. The business rose to modest annual sales of less than $200,000, and showed little capacity to grow rapidly. The founding team concluded that the main problem with their company was them! Subsequently, they found a fourth partner with the key entrepreneurial skills which they lacked. Nine months later they reported sales up by 60% and profits up by 500% and earnings per share doubled.

Selection Criteria

What skills or resources does the venture need, in addition to those of the founder? Are they needed now? Are all of them needed? Are they needed five days per week or less? Can the business afford them? Initially, tax and legal expertise usually can best be obtained part-time. Special expertise may be needed only on a one-time basis—design of an inventory control system, for example. If the need is for a one-time or periodic resource, or is peripheral to the key tasks, goals, and activities required by the business, then the part-time or one-time alternative makes sense.

However, if the expertise is a must for the venture at the outset and the founder cannot provide it, or learn it soon enough, then one or possibly more people will have to be enticed to join the firm. In reality, this usually takes longer than you think.

A small sales, installation and service firm in the private tele-phone-line business grew from $5 million in sales to $16 million in just two years, outgrowing its chief financial officer in the process. How long did it take to find a replacement? Nearly six months!

New team members should complement, not duplicate, the founder's capabilities. Realistically, there will be overlap-ping and sharing responsibilities. Indeed, most new ventures defy simple categorization such as implied by a formal organ-ization chart.

The high levels of uncertainty and very rapid rates of change that characterize the start-up of a new venture require a fluid and highly adaptive form of organization. Such an organization may appear quite amorphous to a manager or engineer accustomed to more highly structured large com-panies. But an organization that can respond quickly and ef-fectively is a must in the heat of start-up. Moreover, man-power is too scarce and too critical in the new venture to en-courage the luxury of duplicate managerial skills.

Team Fit

Like most organizations, new ventures will thrive or wither depending on how well the management team works together. Venture capitalists place heavy importance on the team's ability to work with the investors. The implication of a poor matchup is clear; the venture begins on a shaky foun-dation and probably will not make it. It is critical for the health of the venture that the team be well matched psycho-logically and interpersonally.

The founder has a unique opportunity during the early gestation of a venture to screen potential partners and to measure their commitment, trust, and capabilities. The opportunity is provided in the "moonlighting" phase of most start-ups. The founder and some selected partners may work together on a business plan, develop a prototype, and actually begin forming a corporation, issuing stock and working full-time. This moonlighting phase provides a useful shakedown period for the team and enables the founder to test the commitment and contribution of team members before final decisions on salary and stock are made.

To build a substantial business, the partners must be totally committed to and totally immersed in the venture. Its success must be their most important goal. Other priorities must come second, including families. This total immersion can be observed during the moonlighting phase, through role-playing with team members and through their reactions to such things as heavy work loads, travel, and other sacrifices. The ultimate test is whether partners are prepared to invest their own money and take the full-time plunge.

In early 1988 a quite successful and very experienced entrepreneur visited me with a progress report and fund-raising plan for a new software concept. The demo disk was developed and he was looking for about $1.5 million to launch the company. He was still spread out in his existing company among several client projects, and his partner was working full-time at a large company. The two of them could afford personally to invest another $100,000 to $200,000, but were reluctant to do so. Yet they expected others to invest in two part-timers who would not put more of their own money in their great idea.

It is equally important to encourage each prospective team member to engage in self-assessment before and during the moonlighting phase. These assessments can provide valuable inputs to the evaluation and trust-building process. Deeper understanding of the individual's personal goals, life goals, family goals, and values can greatly facilitate an evaluation of trustworthiness, commitment, and capabilities.

Perhaps most crucial in the team formation process is creating realistic expectations for new team members. The founder can be highly influential in helping to establish a viable psychological contract and a climate of trust and straightforwardness. Moreover, by an example of total immersion the founder can encourage greater commitment, higher standards of excellence, and mutual respect for the expertise the members contribute.

Align Expectations and Realities

As noted previously, team members must complement the founder's strengths. This involves identifying potential fits between tasks and responsibilities to be performed and each person's expertise and capabilities. A diligent effort should be made to determine who has what responsibility for key tasks and problems during start-up.

Such roles cannot be precisely pinned down for all tasks, since some key tasks and problems simply cannot be anticipated, and the actual contributions are not always made by people originally expected to make them. Indeed, maintaining a loose structure with shared responsibility and information is probably desirable for flexibility, rapid learning, and responsive decision making. Therefore, some flexibility must be left for reviewing and revising these alignments.

Often outside advisers and board members can provide useful insights into this ongoing endeavor. Usually, each team member will wear several hats, but the keys seem to be: minimize unnecessary duplication of capability or responsibility, have team members in a role or job they are most comfortable with, and allow team members to share or even rotate responsibility. The net effect of this approach is to encourage informal sharing of problems and information, while utilizing individual strengths. In addition, this flexibility tends to enable individuals to seize neglected problems and to respond quickly to changing needs and demands.

One area that can easily be overlooked is the risk-taking orientation of the team as a whole. Successful entrepreneurs appear to be calculated, moderate risk-takers, and some teams have found it helpful to have a more conservative, lower-risk-taking person on the team. Such caution can help offset the tendency of overly optimistic and competitive team members to overlook certain events, or to overestimate other events, such as sales forecasts.

The message of all this is straightforward: discussing these issues—before starting up—is the least expensive, yet most valuable, insurance policy you can own.

Courtship, Marriage and Family

The marriage analogy is a useful one for examining the process of forming an entrepreneurial team. Forming a venture team has many of the characteristics of the courtship and marriage ritual. It involves decisions based in part on emotion, or "gut" feeling. There may be among partners admiration, respect, and often fierce loyalty—an infatuation with one another. Similarly, the complex psychological joys, frustrations, and uncertainties that accompany most marriages are experienced in entrepreneurial teams as well. For instance, will the new product have a successful introduction (birth), will it be healthy and grow, will we have more, will we survive the strains of raising these products (children)?

A Word About Trust

Trust raises another of the many paradoxes of entre-preneurship. Integrity is very important in long-term busi-ness success. Yet anyone who knows the real world knows it is full of predators, crooks, frauds, and imposters. You can-not succeed without trust, but you cannot succeed with blind or naive trust either.

Trust is something that is earned, usually slowly—and one thoughtless incident can shatter it. This is why investors prefer to see a team that has worked closely together over a period of time.

What do you do to establish trust? Work hard at earning and building it, and even harder to preserve it once you've found it. When you have found a partner you trust, you have found something invaluable, that no money can buy. Hold on to it dearly. Have patience: it takes more than a few weeks or months for most relationships to develop trust. Rely on your instincts and gut feel: if you, or your spouse or partners don't feel right about the person, back off, or find a way out.

As for outsiders and new relationships: a little cynicism can go a long way. Why proceed blindly and naively? Have you signed agreements, documents or other contractual obli-gations without fully investigating (called "due diligence") the person or firm? If the commitments and obligations turn sour or downright disastrous, have you arranged to protect yourself?

Unfortunately, there are more than enough predators out there, just waiting for the innocent. If you are unprepared and unprotected, you will in all likelihood become their vic-tim. In so many aspects of entrepreneuring, the "devil is in the details!" Unless you do the homework, and digest the de-tails *yourself*, you may pay a high price.

The dilemma constantly faced by entrepreneurs is the crunch of real time. There may invariably be more compelling priorities to attend to, but failing to pay attention to such details as discussed here can be punishing. Consider the following example:

A young entrepreneur was extremely busy building his part of an international computer-related business. His attorney suggested he look at a tax-sheltered real-estate investment. Since he did not have the time himself, he trusted the attorney, since the attorney had done satisfactory work for him previously, and was one of the general partners of the deal. He also reasoned that since he was now earning in excess of $100,000 a year, at age 30, it was time to get other professionals to help him manage his money. After all, his time was better spent on building the business and making money. He never thoroughly read and analyzed the prospectus on the deal. Even if he had, he claimed it would not have mattered: he trusted the attorney.

Sadly, the tale does not end happily. The young entrepreneur is likely to lose all, or most, of a $150,000 investment. His attorney is embroiled in numerous lawsuits for mismanagement of the general partnership. The young man and the other limited partners will sue the attorney for malpractice, among other things. In hindsight, perhaps a little patience and cynicism would have helped.

Reference Groups and Potential Partners

One easily overlooked aspect of the team creation process is the entrepreneur's source of social and psychological support and reinforcement. Reference groups—groups in which values and interests are shared, with whom there is frequent interaction (family, friends, co-workers), and from whom is derived support and approval for activities—have long been known for their influence on behavior.

Decisions of all sorts are influenced by the opinions of those persons sought for advice, and whose feedback is respected, on such issues as college choice, career choice, or involvement in community affairs. The entrepreneur leads a lonely existence as it is, and acceptance or rejection by a reference group can have an appreciable effect on long-term commitment.

Such information takes time to gather and can be difficult to obtain. Working with a prospective partner for six months or more is clearly more valuable. But some basic influences are worth noting when assessing a prospective team member:

Does the spouse think entrepreneurship is a great idea, and is behind it 100%? If no other sources of capital are available and the venture needs it, would a second mortgage on the house be tolerable to the spouse? Does the spouse accept the "sweat equity" required during the moonlighting phase? The new venture team faces heavy psychological burdens. If spouse and family are not supportive, the team member may not have the sustained commitment needed when adversity strikes.

What about close friends, the people the partner socializes with and enjoys leisure time with? How do they feel about someone crazy enough to give up "the good life," risk savings, and help start a business? Are these people a source of support and encouragement, or of detraction and negativism?

Knowing something of a prospective team member's reference groups can provide useful insights into the commitment to be expected. The support should be there—if it is not, the founder may have to accept the additional "cheer leader" burden of encouraging and support-ing the team member in hard times.

Renewing and Keeping the Team Together

Selecting and building a team is continual. Constant and rapid changes during start-up and the difficult early going require perpetual vigil over team progress and problems. The venture cannot survive sluggishness or ineffectiveness by any team member.

Will even an ideal team stay together for long? Richard Testa, a leading business attorney whose firm deals with start-ups and high-potential ventures (including Lotus Development of 1-2-3 fame) remarked at a gathering of entrepreneurs, "The only thing that I can tell you with great certainty about this start-up business has to do with you and your partners. I can virtually guarantee you, based on our decade plus of experience, that five years from now at least one of the founders will have left every company represented here today."

Given the hectic turmoil of start-up ventures today, the eventual breakup of the founding team is virtually certain. What can be done about it? It is essential to determine that everyone is committed to the same goal. For ambitious entrepreneurs selecting more than just a lifestyle venture or job substitute, the goal is clear: to realize a substantial capital gain in the next five to ten years. All the stock ownership, incentives and rewards should be aimed at reinforcing this goal. If you have another goal, fine—as long as the team members know and agree on what they want out of the venture.

Vesting Stock Ownership

In recent years new mechanisms have emerged to foster longer term commitment to the success of the venture, while at the same time providing a method for a civilized, "no-fault" corporate divorce. The mechanism used in start-ups is a stock vesting agreement, which is attached as a restriction on the "unregistered" stock certificate. Typically, the vesting agreement establishes a period of years, often four or more, during which the founding stockholders can "earn out" their shares.

If a member of the founding team decides to leave the company prior to completing the vesting period, he or she may be required to sell the stock back to the company for the price originally paid for it, usually nil. The departing shareholder, in this instance, would not own any stock after the departure. Nor would any capital-gain windfall be realized. In other cases, founders may vest a certain portion each year, so they have some shares even if they leave. Such vesting can be weighted toward the last year or two of the vesting period.

Other common restrictions on this "unregistered stock" give management and the board control over the disposition of it, whether or not the stockholder stays or leaves the company. In effect, the founders and board have to approve the sale of the stock, the terms, and the buyer. This, of course, is generally in the interest of the founders and any original outside investors.

In essence, this mechanism confronts the founder-shareholder with the reality that the venture is not a "get rich quick" exercise. Anyone considering joining the venture will have to take it seriously, and be highly committed, in order to accept such terms. And for the lead entrepreneur such requirements can help sort out any prospects lacking the appropriate motivation and commitment. Further, it prevents the possibility of the new company being exploited by a departing shareholder who seeks an outrageous price for his or her stock or, failing to come to terms, resorts to litigation.

Indeed, the mechanism places the reward structure exactly where it should be: on successfully building the business and realizing a capital gain. That necessitates a long-term, serious commitment. And unless all the founders are convinced it is really going to succeed, these vesting realities may cause them to think twice, and to abandon what might otherwise become another marginal venture, loaded with personal loan guarantees, and one that is not likely to be harvested.

Solving Team Problems

Issues in a new venture relating to titles, salary, stock and responsibilities can become explosive. Often, intra-team discussions of them may lead to a premature disbanding of promising teams with sound business ideas simply because they lack the skill and knowledge to deal with such thorny issues. Poorly conceived approaches, with a faint consensus and hesitant commitment by some team members, will only lead to post-start-up blues for all concerned.

A competent outside counselor or advisor with a lot of common sense and a knack for dealing with people problems and new ventures can help team members reason out their differences and develop a legitimate consensus. Occasionally, you will find someone who is professionally trained as a psychologist or counselor who has had extensive experience working with presidents and partners in emerging firms.

Because each venture is unique, it is preferable for team members to reach a reasoned decision for themselves concerning sensitive issues, rather than try to apply some predetermined model. An essential first step is to recognize the various factors which should influence their decisions on such matters as ownership and salaries: for example, who generated the idea for the venture, who provided the sweat equity and expertise, the track records of team members relative to the needs of the business, the extent of their potential contributions to the firm's goals, the dollars that each has available to invest personally, and the effort each has contributed in preparing the business plan.

There is need for an extended "mating dance" among potential partners, preferably during a "moonlighting" period prior to actually launching the venture. Probably the best single source of this "getting-to-know-you" process is having worked closely together in another company on a common goal or project. This courtship should be tested thoroughly before ownership and other commitments are solidified, as these are very difficult and costly to alter or revoke once established. Preparing the business plan, discussing and presenting it to potential investors, working on a prototype, and dealing with other prospective team members should all provide unique opportunities to test the potential marriage.

No matter how much time is devoted to team-building tasks, chances are high that agreements will become obsolete. Within four to seven years—if not sooner—the initially agreed-upon salaries and stock positions are unlikely to reflect the actual contributions by each team member to the venture's success. Internal adjustments will be required as the venture grows if stock and salary rewards are to reflect actual performances by team members.

Conclusion

The focus here has been on developing a framework for easing the burden of team formation and development. Obviously, it is time-consuming and demanding to work through the process. The impatience of most entrepreneurs mitigates against a long, drawn-out process. Some might handle these issues on an intuitive basis and do quite well. But each element needs to be considered carefully during preparation of the business plan and during the early life of the venture. The order, emphasis and effort need not match precisely the framework presented here, but to ignore these issues invites eventual disaster. For the patient and careful founder, this framework should help in the analysis of the relevant issues and serve as an aid to individual decision making. And the payoff for creating a highly effective team from the outset can be very substantial.

Finally, the focus has been on pre-start-up and early start-up phases of the venture. As a venture matures, the needs, demands, and requirements of the business change. Continual review of each of these critical elements is also appropriate as these new stages of growth are encountered.

Evaluation and selection of team members are some of the most difficult decisions an entrepreneur must make. There will always be some doubt, hope for more than the prospective partner can deliver, and constant reassessment. Eventually, the choice must be made, and the tests of time and working together should prevail.

10

Building the
New Venture Team

The critical ingredients in team building and formation previously described lay the foundation for a new venture team. This foundation building is a continuous process, as the requirements of the venture for managerial and entrepreneurial talent change over time. The distinctions between forming and building the team are conceptual, since in practice the two overlap. It is never too early to begin conscious team-building efforts. [1]

The needs and demands of a start-up situation are complex and constantly, rapidly evolving. It is nearly impossible to anticipate all the needs. Yet research, experience, and practical observation indicate some useful concepts for building effective new-venture teamwork, including organizational climate, teamwork and interpersonal skills, and helping skills.

The cumulative net effect of managing each of these aspects of the venture well is to create psychological contracts, realistic expectations, and trust among the venture partners.

Organizational Culture

The concept of organizational climate or culture has been used for some time to study performance in large business

1 *INC.*, *Venture* and *In Business* magazines usually contain very useful and informative articles about partners and teams and the issues and challenges they face in launching and building their businesses.

organizations. A number of completed studies lead to three general conclusions: (1) The "culture" of an organization (the perceptions of people as to the kind of place it is to work in) have significant impact on performance. (2) Climate is created both by the expectations people bring to the organization and the practices and attitudes of the key managers. (3) Managers can create high-performance climates or they can create climates that foster mediocrity or doom.

The climate construct has relevance for new ventures as well. What, then, should venture founders know about organizational climate, and how can this knowledge contribute to effective team building and venture performance? There are six basic dimensions for describing the climate of an organization. Each of these dimensions is important for high performance. What management practices and priorities correlate well with them to create a positive climate?

Clarity Is the firm well organized—concise and efficient in the way tasks, procedures, and assignments are made and accomplished? Goal setting, task and project assignment, problem solving and informal interaction enhance clarity.

Standards Does management expect and put pressure on employees for excellent performance? Goal setting, individual and group meetings on standards and providing feedback help keep standards high.

Commitment Do employees feel committed to the goals and objectives of the organization? Goal setting, task and project assignment, problem solving and informal interaction help strengthen commitment.

Responsibility Do members of the organization feel individual responsibility for accomplishing their goals without being constantly monitored and second-guessed? Individual and group meetings and providing feedback foster feelings of responsibility.

Recognition Do employees feel they are recognized and rewarded with money for a job well done, or only punished for mistakes or errors? Task and project assignment, group meetings, providing feedback and engaging in informal interaction heighten the sense of recognition.

Cohesion Do employees feel part of a team that works well together? Again, task and project assignment, group meetings, providing feedback and engaging in informal interaction strengthen teamwork.

In addition, it is helpful to examine how these aspects of climate generally influence an organization's performance and health, since all aspects may not have equal priority for the venture team:

Clarity affects adaptation.

Standards affect return on investment and profit performance.

Commitment affects growth performance.

Responsibility and recognition affect individual development

Cohesion affects group efficiency and effectiveness.

Teamwork and Interpersonal Skills

Most of us have had an unpleasant experience with another person—a salesclerk, a waiter, or other—where we later remarked, "It wasn't so much what he or she said, but rather how it was said, that blew my stack." Knowledge about the teamwork process—how groups work well together—can be applied to managing a venture team.

One team exercise in particular—the NASA Space Survival Exercise—is helpful in identifying effective team-building behaviors. It is a problem-solving exercise in which individuals rank items in order of their importance for survival on the moon, first by themselves and then as a team.

Superior teams in this exercise operate differently than poorly performing teams in terms of listening and participation, roles performed by team members, resolving leadership issues, using team resources, dealing with disagreements, setting priorities, and establishing a climate.

These results are relevant for many of the problem-solving and decision-making situations experienced by new venture teams. Furthermore, they can be learned and used by venture founders and team members to facilitate problem-solving. These skills or orientations might also be sought when selecting venture team members. Ideally, technical or managerial competence should be accompanied by a capacity to work well with a team.

Team Process Skills

Priorities Effective teams usually seek a method and criteria for solving problems at outset, rather than "dive in." They are aware of time limitations.

Ineffective teams use the alligator technique—they jump in with arms and legs and jaws in motion, rarely asking: What's a good way to solve the problem? How should we go about it, given time constraints? What resources do we have in the team? What criteria are relevant?

Climate Effective: respect for other's opinions; open to criticism and differences of opinion; little sarcasm or put-downs, an atmosphere that encourages thinking, discussion, reasoning, and getting the job done. Willingness to listen and change minds.

Ineffective: members are either very friendly or hostile; jovial members don't take task seriously, wish only to avoid conflict; hostiles are full of sarcasm and put-downs which tend to make other members clam up; bullies force their solutions. Unwilling to change minds.

Leadership Effective: elected leaders are accepted as legitimate but don't force their solutions; leadership may be shared, or informal or "natural" leader may guide task; time not wasted in competing for leadership; based on expertise—not authority.

Ineffective: competition for who will lead team among two or three members; a self-appointed, dominant, and aggressive person may take over. Leader tends to force own solution on team, doesn't seek involvement of potential resources.

Roles Effective: emphasis on performing task-oriented roles, but someone invariably provides for "maintenance" and group cohesion by good humor and wit.

Ineffective: Absence of task or maintenance roles; domination by one member is typical.

Participation/Listening Effective: circular seating arrangements are chosen intuitively and facilitate balanced interaction; balanced participation utilizes all team resources; members listen well, with few interruptions or side conversations; functional interruptions only to avoid waste of time on irrelevant points. Discussion is usually calm, quiet.

Ineffective: many interruptions, loud conversations, sometimes shouting; subgroups often engage in conversation; members unwilling to listen to others or alter individual views.

Conflict Resolution Effective: open confrontation of differences of opinion; logic and reason tend to prevail; members less emotional, willing to talk out differences, assumptions, reasons, inferences, and willing to change opinion based on consensus (as a jury does) or near unanimous majority (six or seven must agree). The confrontations can involve considerable emotion.

Ineffective: usually emotional and loud; much argument rather than reasoning; members tend to want to avoid conflict or differences by compromising, voting, trading-off; show stubborn attachment to individual solutions. Simple majority vote used to resolve conflict.

Two additional factors can also have a significant impact on teamwork. First, *trust* is essential. Second, the process is enhanced by *compatibility* of team members, especially in terms of goals, values, commitment, life styles and work style. As was noted earlier, the goals of a new venture generally reflect the values and personal needs of the founder and key members. The greater the sources of conflict over philosophical issues, which tend to be extremely time-consuming and exhausting to resolve, the more energy is directed away from the primary aims of the venture. Such differences can erode the foundations of good teamwork.

Helping Skills

It is difficult to think of a successful team in any field whose members don't feel that they are helped a great deal by their teammates. This help usually comes in the form of coaching to improve technical skills or providing psychological support and reinforcement. Giving and receiving help are skills increasingly acknowledged as important aspects of effective managing. The limited resources of most new ventures make helping skills especially critical for members of the entrepreneurial team.

Helping skills involve two distinct elements: willingness and ability to seek and to receive help from others, and willingness and ability to give help to others. Both of these skills are at the core of effective working and consultative relationships. The helping process can be viewed in terms of the task to be accomplished, the motives and self-image of the giver and receiver of help, the psychological climate in which the process takes place, and the feedback that occurs.

The following summation offers bench marks for practicing and improving helping skills. An outside consultant can assist by observing and providing feedback.

A receiver of help can assist the process by articulating the problem, asking for help, believing that the giver can help, trusting the giver, being open and honest, being receptive to help, finding a helper who cares about the problem, and being a good listener. The receiver can hinder it by being rigidly attached to his definition of the problem, being unwilling to reexamine the problem, having hostile expectations, and being a poor listener.

A giver of help can assist the process by creating a positive climate, using nonverbal cues, listening effectively, asking probing questions, and focusing on what the receiver can do. The giver can hinder it by prejudging the problem or solution, not listening, and taking over the problem.

Common Pitfalls

A lead entrepreneur whose self-assessment leads him to believe that he can become an effective team player has the greatest potential for success by avoiding three common pitfalls:

The Leaderless Democracy This is what has sometimes been termed the "commune approach" to forming a new venture team. Two to four entrepreneurs, usually friends or work acquaintances, decide to initiate a venture or buy out a small company together, demonstrating their equality with such democratic trimmings as equal stock ownership, equal salaries, equal office space and cars, and other items symbolizing their peer status.

Anyone who has lived through such an investment knows well the problems that this myopic approach fosters. There is no pecking order, so who's in charge? Who makes the final decisions and how long does it take? How are real differences of opinion resolved without early-defined leadership roles? While some role overlapping and a sharing and negotiating of decisions is desirable in new venture teams, too much looseness is debilitating. Even sophisticated buy-sell agreements among partners often fail to resolve the conflicts.

The Unexamined Leader You need to know what you do and do not know in order to form a strong team. If you don't know or admit to your deficiencies and weaknesses, you won't be likely to complement them by adding team members who are strong in those areas. You also should understand what is really needed to make a new venture grow beyond a million-dollar business. Technically-oriented people or those without experience in the business they wish to launch often lack this understanding.

The principal entrepreneur may be overly fascinated with his own product or idea. Although an emotional attachment to one's brainchild may be essential to generate enthusiasm and commitment, it can also cloud the realities of what it takes to build a substantial business. A first-rate idea or product without a first-rate entrepreneurial team has little appeal to the investor. Overcommitment to any idea usually leads to problems.

The Power-Oriented Leader Whether you are an investor, prospective team member, or lead entrepreneur, it is important to be alert to potentially destructive motivation. Early concern for power and control and heavy expenditures on the symbols of status and prestige—such as luxury automobiles, lavish entertainment, and plush offices—is a danger signal. Entrepreneurs who derive their satisfaction in this way rarely build rapidly growing firms.

In contrast, the entrepreneurs with an achievement orientation focus on the goal of building a substantial business and approach each new hurdle or disagreement with team members as a problem to be solved, rather than as a new round of negotiations to be won or lost.

11

Rewarding the
New Venture Team

One of the most important issues to be faced and managed effectively by new venture teams is how each member of the team is to be rewarded. [1] The apportioning of compensation within the team strongly affects the satisfaction of each team member, and the division of equity between the internal team and external investors will affect how much of the venture's equity is available to the team.

The financial rewards of a venture—and this includes stock, salary, and fringes—are part of a larger reward system that includes the chance to realize personal goals, exercise autonomy, and develop skills in particular venture roles. To a great extent, being able to attract and keep high-quality team members depends on these financial and psychological rewards. Because these rewards are so important, and an early-stage venture is limited in what it can offer, the total reward system should be thought through very carefully.

When you begin deciding who gets how many shares of stock, who gets how many dollars of salary, and who gets what fringe benefits, a number of difficult issues arise. How should these distributions be made? What criteria are appropriate? What time-tested formulas can you turn to?

The democracy or commune approach can work, but it involves higher risk and more pitfalls than one that

1 I am indebted to John L. Hayes and the late Brian Haslett of Venture Founders Corporation for their major contribution and permission to use it here.

differentiates value among the team members. Each team member rarely contributes the same amount to the venture, and the reward system should recognize these differences.

Also, regardless of the contribution of each team member at any moment, the probability is high that the contribution will change over time. One team member may perform substantially more or less than anticipated; a team member may have to be replaced; an additional team member may have to be recruited and added to the existing team. Many ventures have been torn apart when the relative contributions of the team members changed dramatically several years after start-up without a significant change in the stock split.

More important is the process by which the split is decided, and the willingness of each team member to confront the issues openly when decisions have to be made. It is this commitment to dealing with the issue which will assure that rewards continue to reflect contributed performance.

That which is actually perceived as a reward by any single team member will vary, depending upon personal values, goals and aspirations. Some may seek long-range capital gains while other desire more security and shorter-range income. Before any apportioning of rewards is decided, it is important to identify what each team member really wants.

Timing of Rewards

The rewards a venture is able to give vary over the life of the venture. A division of stock among the members of the team will be decided very early in the life of the venture. Some of the financial rewards are more or less appropriate at different stages of the venture's development. The intangible rewards like opportunity for self-development and realization may be available throughout the life of a venture.

Once the initial allocation is decided, the relative stock

positions of team members will not change, unless there are significant changes in contribution. New team members or an external investor might dilute the team's position, but the relative individual positions will probably remain the same. Because the founding stock is likely to increase greatly in value, it is extremely important that the allocations reflect a best estimate of contributed performance over the first several years of the venture.

Take, for example, four young engineers who started a computer terminal company in the late 1970s as equal partners. Three years later two of them were contributing about 110% of the success of the company, one about 30%, and one minus 40%. Outside investors were prepared to invest $1 million in the company if ownership were realigned to reflect the real contributions of the founders. The partners who were not carrying their weight would not agree to this, thus killing the deal and permanently injuring the company.

There are several events that may occur during the early years that have implications for initial stock assignments: (1) A team member, who has a substantial portion of your company's stock, does not perform and must be replaced a year into the venture. (2) A key team member finds a better opportunity and quits after a year. (3) A key team member dies a year into the venture.

What will happen to the stock of these team members in each of the above cases? The stock was intended to be a reward for the performance of the team member during the first several years. In Case 1, the venture should have the option of returning the stock to its treasury for the purchase price—that was the team member's commitment and risk. In Cases 2 and 3, some portion of the stock has been earned and some as yet unearned. Any arrangement here needs to be carefully thought out to do justice to all parties. In Case 3, the heirs of the deceased partner must be considered.

To protect the company against the negative effects of such occurrences, several options are available when the initial stock allocations are made. Once purchased by the team members, stock may be placed in escrow and then be released over a two- or three-year period. This provides a continuing reward for team members. Another option is to structure buy-back agreements that allow the company to repurchase stock under specific circumstances. Whatever mechanism is used, the objective is to avoid the loss or freezing of equity the business needs to reward real performers.

Other rewards—salary, stock options, bonus, fringe benefits—can be manipulated more readily to reflect changes in performance. But their use depends upon the stage of development of the venture. In the early months, salaries will be low or nonexistent, and bonuses and fringe benefits are out of the question. They all drain cash from the business. Until profitability is achieved, cash must be put toward operations. Even after profitability is achieved, cash payments will still limit growth. Salaries can become competitive once the venture has passed breakeven, but bonuses and fringe benefits should be kept at a minimum until several years of profitability have been demonstrated. Even then, the owners of the venture will be trading off cash rewards and the growth of the venture.

Valuing Performance

When an entrepreneur or entrepreneurial team is attempting to decide a fair division of stock among team members, various aspects of contribution and performance should be identified and weighed, including:

Contribution to the idea—
>   Whose idea was it?
>   What was the amount of "sweat equity" contributed to it?
>   Are trade secrets or special technology involved?
>   Was a prototype developed?
>   Has research on product or market been done?

Dollars and hours expended in preparing the business plan—
Degree of risk and commitment—
>   What alternatives were foregone and what is their value?
>   What percent of net worth is invested in the company?
>   What is risked if the company fails?
>   What personal sacrifices have been made?
>   Willing to put in long hours and major effort?
>   Reputation at risk?
>   Reduced salary accepted as measure of commitment?
>   How much time has been spent already?

Skills brought to the venture (marketing, technical, financial, etc.)—
>   How important are the skills?
>   Are the skills readily available from outside?
>   Have experience in area of new venture?
>   Have track record?

Number of contacts of value to the venture—
Responsibility taken in the venture—
>   Importance of role to venture success.

Contribution to the idea and to the business plan are frequently overvalued in stock negotiations. In terms of the real success of the venture three to five years down the road, it is difficult to justify much more than 15 to 20 percent for these two items.

Commitment, skills, and responsibility are by far the larger values producing venture success. Exactly what each is worth must be decided intelligently by every new venture. The above list of considerations should be applied to each team member to attempt to arrive at some fair weight of relative contribution. Each of these elements has some value; it is up to your team to agree to these values and to leave the agreements flexible enough to allow changes.

Remember—it is the contribution over a period of several years that you are attempting to predict and reward. If you predict wrongly, make sure that the venture's capacity to reward can be modified. The reward is buying skills, commitment, and concern, and your venture will need all it can get.

Rewards and Outside Investment

The way you deal with these questions will also determine your credibility to the investor. The investor will look for signs of commitment, like reduced salary and stock in escrow pending demonstrated performance; for a fringe-benefit plan that does not strain a young business; for flexibility in the team so that, if necessary, a team member can be replaced. Many venture capitalists have faced the task of replacing the lead entrepreneur or a key team member. and you must convince your investor that your venture could survive such a change.

Conclusion

Reward issues are difficult to resolve. The stakes for each individual are high, and each person's feelings of self-worth are tied to reward. Care must be employed to avoid rigid bargaining positions, and the issues must be confronted and resolved in order to develop a strong, committed entrepreneurial team.

12

The Family Venture

by Wendy C. Handler*

Family businesses are very popular today. "All over the country, the bright young types who formerly opted for management consulting or the fast track at blue-chip corporations are eagerly joining family businesses ... Changed attitudes and a changing economy account for this turnaround." (*Business Week*, July 1, 1985). People are tired of bureaucracy, and have turned to family ventures in hopes of success, security, and humanistic work values. However, many are finding that the complexities of putting together a venture team are compounded when family members and other relatives become involved in the business.

Historically, the family's involvement in business has been the least understood aspect of new venture creation. Yet, of the more than 18 million businesses in the U.S., nine out of ten are family-dominated. Family firms range in size from small local stores to large multinational corporations, and produce half the gross national product.

Family members may become involved in a venture at one of three stages:

1. At start-up (or buy-out) as a partner or member of the entrepreneurial team.

2. Joining a recently launched family venture early in its operation.

* The author teaches family business management at Boston University's School of Management, and has researched succession in family firms from the perspective of next-generation family members.

3. Joining a family business anytime during the life of the organization as a second or third generation member.

Launching a Venture with a Family Member

Everything that has been said about choosing entrepreneurial teams and practicing teamwork applies to new family ventures. There are also special advantages: Initial costs and early losses may be more easily shared, and later success benefits the family as a whole. It also enables the family to be together, one of the major reasons couples choose to go into business with one another. One form of partnership that has gained popularity in the 1980s is the enterprise owned and run by a married couple.

Cheryl and Jeffrey Katz of Boston insist that they would rather work with each other than anyone else. Their design studio allows them to fulfill a mutual interest together. Bridget and Greg Martin, owners of an ice cream shop, believe that their business is so all-consuming that it would be difficult for them if they did not both work there. They both have enthusiasm about the business, so neither minds if the other wants to talk about work.

Couples may have certain benefits that are atypical of nonfamily partnerships, because they share the same family needs. If a child is sick and must stay home from school, the couple makes the necessary business adjustments so that one parent can be at home. Many couples deal with the equity issue by agreeing that there is no single "boss." Major decisions, especially financial, are made together, while smaller ones depend on who is available. [1]

1 R. O'Gorman Flynn, "For Love and Money," *Boston Woman*, June 1987.

Family members may also trust one another more than they do people outside the family. The issue of trust is paramount in the wholesale diamond business, as one member of a family firm in that industry explained it: "Dealing with diamonds is basically a family business, because you're dealing with these small things that are very expensive, and you must have a lot of trust in whoever you work with. So you don't hire [nonfamily] salesmen."

A family partnership can work well when the partners have abilities and responsibilities that complement each other, like brothers Ernest and Julio of Gallo Vineyards.

Ernest, 77, is chairman and in charge of marketing, sales and distribution. Julio, 76, is president and oversees production. Julio describes himself as a farmer at heart, who likes to "walk in the fields with the old-timers." Ernest's office, on the other hand, is cluttered with mementos from selling. The brothers mesh well: Julio's goal is to make more wine than Ernest can sell. Ernest's goal is to sell more wine than Julio can make. [2]

But partnerships can turn sour when a business partner or boss is also a relative. This may also have serious implications for family relationships. Problems of control, fairness, and equity are common. Conflicts over control result when each partner has a different idea of how to run the business, and both are unwilling to compromise. Issues of fairness and equity arise over division of work and how much each partner is contributing to profit. And, in a business run by a couple, difficulties in the personal relationship may undermine the business.

2 J. Fierman, "How Gallo Crushes the Competition," *Fortune*, Sept. 1, 1986.

Esprit, *the billion-dollar international clothing company, has experienced plummeting sales, largely blamed on founder-owners Doug and Susie Tompkins being "at each other's throat," according to* Newsweek *magazine (May 23, 1988). They moved into separate buildings on their estate overlooking San Francisco Bay.*

They disagree as well about the future direction of the company. She wants to produce more mature clothes for the aging baby boomers, while he insists on sticking with the youth market. In May of 1988, to placate concerned stockholders, the couple agreed to reorganize the company, and have given up some of their personal control of it.

If you are thinking about going into business with one or more members of your family, it is important to understand that you are entering a business relationship. Make adequate plans for managing its future. It is fatal to the life of a venture to assume that these issues are "understood" because "it's all in the family."

Of special urgency is the need to have a clear understanding about the following issues:

Who (if anyone) is the lead entrepreneur?

What are the specific strengths and weaknesses of each member of the team?

What are the backgrounds of each in other areas of business?

What are the specific responsibilities of each?

How much money will each put up, and how will equity be divided?

Often family members in business together have trouble communicating honestly and willingly with one another. It is important that differences of opinion about the business be discussed in a professional manner. Regular meetings to take up day-to-day matters and longer range plans are a good idea.

Finally, the family must decide under what circumstances, and on what terms, nonfamily will be brought into the venture. While keeping a venture strictly in the family ensures complete control, this approach may also limit growth by discouraging able and potential partners from joining, if the inner circle is closed to them. It may also discourage potential investors who may question the growth potential of a tightly held operation.

Joining a New Family Venture Early in its Operation

A typical scenario for joining a new family venture early might be an entrepreneur who starts small, with the understanding that a sibling (employed elsewhere or still in school) or a parent will join the venture as it grows. In this instance, the lead entrepreneur has already declared himself or herself, and presumably has identified the areas in which the venture needs the help of potential family partners, employees and backers.

There are various advantages to having family members join a new venture. They can help during the development period. They may welcome the opportunity to help the business because it benefits the family. Flexible hours and days (and pay) may be attractive to family members struggling to get the business going while using minimum resources. Working together also enables the family to be together.

One member of a family that owns a successful restaurant chain in Boston talked about his father's desire to have the family together in business: "He wanted to have his family around—I think that was one of his greatest priorities. We went to school in different places and we did different kinds of things. Each one of us moved away for a little while. But his goal always was, as well as

my mother's goal always was, to have the family close by ... because he
looks at a lot of people he knows and the kids are all over the country, all
over the world, and maybe they're successful, but the parents never see
them ...."

Many family members join a family business because they are uncomfortable with close supervision, or with working in a bureaucratic atmosphere—and are welcomed because family members are typically more trustworthy and responsible (or seen as so) than outsiders.

A woman's specialty clothing shop in Boston is run by two sisters,
ten years apart in age. The younger sister started working for the older
sister because it gave her autonomy without working alone. The older
sister is happy because she thinks family is more reliable and cares more
about the business.

The problems of a family business early in its operation are largely interpersonal. An entrepreneur employing a parent may experience role reversal, which can be awkward, given the history of relating as a son or daughter. The parent may be resentful, if the work is unrewarding, tedious or difficult.

In the case of siblings, issues of power, rivalry and jealousy may crop up if the relationship is not carefully managed—especially if they are close in age and of the same gender. It is important to delineate areas of responsibility clearly, and they should be based on personal interest, skills and training.

For the case of family members joining a venture early in its operation, therefore, many issues must be worked out:
What, exactly, is the area of responsibility of each family member, and to whom is he or she responsible?

What is the compensation: salary, bonus, equity shares, or
some mixture?
What will be done in the event of a disagreement, or if one
family member is not pulling his/her weight?
What is the ante—can it be redeemed if the joining family
member changes his mind?

Discussion of questions like these are best done in periodic family meetings, so that the experience of working in the
family business is beneficial and productive.

Joining a Family Company as a Later Generation Member

Joining a family company as a later generation member is
probably the most common path—and is filled with stories of
success and failure. Thomas Watson Jr., for example, "got his
job from his father, but built IBM into a colossus big enough
to satisfy even the wildest of the old man's dreams." [3]   In
contrast are the Bingham heirs of Louisville, Kentucky,
whose squabbling led to the downfall and sale of a $400 mill-
ion media empire.

There are three broad categories of next-generation members of a family firm, described below. Which category an
individual "fits" depends on personal qualities, interests, and
needs. Furthermore, the decision to join a family venture is
subtle and dynamic, and can take many years and several
periods in and out of the business to solidify.

*A woman actively involved in her family's printing business
talked about her tenuous existence during the early years: "There
was a lot of aggravation. I quit twenty times. [My father] fired me
twenty times. I fired him twenty times. We fired each other—we
both walked out. We were gonna close the whole place."*

3 "The Greatest Capitalist in History," *Fortune*, August 31, 1987.

The Helper or Faithful Apprentice. The helper is the individual who joins to help out in the organization, and is often unsure how long his or her tenure will be. Often the helper joins at the early stages of development, when the entrepreneur may rely heavily on family members for flexible work hours and pay.

Sometimes the helper stays on as the dutiful apprentice to learn the business "from the bottom up." The helper or apprentice may not have a regular title or position, but is expected to be a factotum—someone who does all kinds of work.

Perhaps the best example of the dutiful apprentice is Edsel Ford, only son of the original Henry Ford and father of Henry II, who even as president of Ford Motor Company found himself overshadowed by his father, the real power in the company.

Author Booton Herndon explains how "Edsel stayed on (after his brother-in-law was edged out) under continued harassment and continued to make recommendations for improvements.... On one occasion, he was recommending to a large group of executives a hydraulic braking system to replace the less efficient mechanical brakes when the old man suddenly turned to him and rasped, 'Edsel, you shut up!' Why did he take it? Two reasons. One, he was a loyal son. He loved his father. Two, he was a Ford, with that awful burden on his shoulders." 4

Nevertheless, one of the benefits of being the helper or faithful apprentice is that you are helping the family. The son of the founder of an industrial development firm said this was what he liked about working for his father:

---

4   B. Herndon, *Ford: An Unconventional Biography of the Men and Their Times.*

"You're contributing to the family, you're helping reach a goal, you're getting something done that needs to be done, you can see progress on the work that you're doing, which is always nice when you're doing work. But I think that the underlying thing is that it's our business. This is what we do, this something that my father does. That kind of attitude or thought process is the main thing that made me want to work for him more and work hard."

There is also the added incentive to help out when there are direct benefits as a member of the family. The young man above noted that his college expenses were affordable because of the family business.

The Stepping Stone. Some individuals use the family firm as a stepping stone on a career path. They are interested in it as a convenient career opportunity, a launching pad to other job choices.

Two sons of restauranteur Anthony Athanas, owner of Anthony's Pier 4 in Boston, set up a seafood supply company in Maine, with the intent of having their father be one of their most loyal customers.

Ira Riklis, son of conglomerateur Meshulam Riklis, of Rapid-American Corporation, worked for his father for one year, developing an ulcer and the conviction that the role was not for him. However, the contacts he made enabled him to start a successful company of his own.

There are several benefits to using the family business as a stepping stone. It resolves the Catch-22 confronting beginners—the need to possess work experience to get the job that gives it. It fulfills the feeling of personal obligation members of the next generation are likely to feel toward the family business. Finally, it allows for personal growth, and development of the business skills needed to move into a desirable job or to begin a business.

The Socialized Successor.   This individual joins and becomes socialized into the family business, with the strong likelihood of becoming the next-generation president.

One notable example is the Bechtel Corporation, begun by Warren Bechtel to build railroads. His son Steve Sr. directed the firm into construction of pipelines and nuclear power plants. Today, Steve Jr. heads the $3 billion company, which has further diversified.

Another example: Frederick A. Wang, 37, son of founder An Wang and currently president, chief operating officer and company spokesperson, is credited with getting Wang Laboratories back on its feet by broadening the product line, imposing financial controls, and ensuring on-time delivery of new products (Business Week, Jan. 25, 1988).

The benefits of being socialized into the family business are similar to the benefits of starting a business: the opportunity to be creative, innovative and goal-oriented. Entrepreneurial success within the family business depends to a great extent on company growth. Is there room for the next generation to expand? Is the company growing fast enough to accommodate new ideas, new divisions? Does the management style permit the type of latitude the next generation seeks?

Important Issues That Confront the Next Generation. Three major issues confront the next-generation member of a family firm. First is the classic problem of the owner who can't let go. To many founders, the company is child and lover. The founder cannot stand to relinquish any part of it, and will often deny the successor the training necessary to qualify to take it over.

In addition, parents do not like to take orders from their children; the generation gap is magnified in the setting of the family business. Often the second-generation entrepreneur becomes a permanent person-in-waiting. A survivor of this syndrome describes his good fortune as follows, "Fortunately, my father died one year after I joined the firm."

A seasoned observer summarizes the dilemma: "Dad's successor is an entrepreneur in training. He's expected to be the trail blazer when Dad passes on his machete. He's expected to be independent, yet he is forced to work for one of the most domineering bosses in existence, a successful business owner. To make it worse, the boss is also the successor's father." [5]

A well-known family business consultant explained that the practice of choosing your own successor is "an organizationally hazardous activity that might better be abolished." [6]

Unconsciously, owner-founders may want to prove no one can fill their shoes. Several successors I have spoken to were aware of this dynamic; one in particular was still trying to come to grips with his father's words, "... if anything happens to me, don't think for one minute that you could ever run this business without me."

A second, related issue is establishing credibility. Founding parents have difficulty believing that their children ever grow up. They push their children to enter the business, but then fail to give them responsibility or encouragement. Few

5 L. Danco, *Inside the Family Business*, Center for Family Business, 1980, p. 131.
6 H. Levinson, "Don't Choose Your Own Successor," *Harvard Business Review*, March-April 1971.

next-generation family members appear to be given direct positive feedback about their performance. Typically, they find out from others if the parent thinks they are doing a good job.

Gaining credibility is a slow, gradual dance between parent and child. The parent (particularly the founder) has worked hard and expects the child to do the same. Family often have higher expectations of family members in the firm, with one implication being that *because* they are family, they do not have to praise their work.

A third complication of entering a family business is family dynamics and conflicts. Boundaries should be set between family life and the business, so that tensions from one do not spill over into the other—although this is very difficult, and often impossible, to do.

While family closeness can be a positive feature, certain family patterns can be counterproductive.

One man spoke to me of coming from an "alcoholic family." The family auto dealership had been very successful, but the alcoholic father had never given him the recognition he deserved, because he sought attention for himself as he battled his alcoholism. The son is now in charge, but doubts his abilities because his father had given him so many bad messages. His father also will not give up control or the presidency, even though he no longer has any real responsibilities in the company. [7]

Even more extreme are cases where the family business has been nearly destroyed by family feuds.

[7]   E. Topolnicki, "Family Firms Can Leave the Feuds Behind," *Money*, July 1983.

Cesare Mondavi, founder of Mondavi Vineyards, before he died, mediated disputes between his two sons over running the family's Charles Krug Winery. The sons, Robert and Peter, had been known for fist fights at their grape-shipping plant. By 1972, Robert was suing Peter for his investment in Krug, and being countersued for trying to monopolize the Napa Valley wine industry. In 1978, a California Superior Court judge ordered that Krug be sold. One month before the sale, Peter bought out Robert's share and saved the business from the auction block.

There is little a next-generation family member can do about the owner who can't let go, but there are direct ways of coping with the issues of credibility and family conflict.

Credibility. There are four strategies for dealing with the credibility issue. First, if you are a next-generation family member, express interest in the family business. Do not assume that your parents know that you are interested. It is important to communicate your interest, and discuss goals with your parents. Be direct and forthright about the responsibility you want and what you are capable of. My research clearly indicates that next-generation family members are more likely to achieve for themselves and the business when they are clear about their needs, and communciate them directly to the owner in charge.

Second, take responsibility for your own development. Decide what your personal goals are and how—or if—they are to be met by the family business. Ask yourself:

What are my strengths and what do I need to work on?

What other aspects of the business do I need to learn?

Do I have the qualities to be a leader?

Am I happy working in the business?

Is there anything else I should do to meet my goals?

If you hope to become head of the business, you should learn as much about the business as you can. A leading family business expert suggests an initial learning stage to understand the business better, followed by a specialization stage to acquire a specific skill. Then become a generalist and learn to manage.[8] How appropriate these steps are, however, depends on the nature, complexity, and size of the business.

Third, develop a relationship with a mentor, or with several people who can act as coach, protector, role model, counselor or even friend. It may not be wise to look only to a parent for mentoring because of possible inherent conflict of interest. Parents play many roles with children; they may not want them to grow up, and may have subconscious difficulty accepting this reality. Look to respected individuals outside the family for counseling and long-term developmental support.

Fourth, and most important, acquire practical business experience outside the family business. This helps increase knowledge, experience and confidence. It is also likely to enhance credibility with employees in a family business, who may be skeptical about the qualifications of family members.

A son of the founder of a software marketing and consulting company in New York was adamant about gaining experience elsewhere: "I think it gives you a very narrow perspective on life to go at age 21 into your family business and be there for the rest of your life. I think it limits your exposure; I don't think you can become as broad and as developed an individual if you're involved in one thing for your entire life ...."

8 S. Nelton, "Making Sure the Business Outlasts You," *Nations Business*, January 1986.

Family Conflict. There are three ways to minimize the likelihood of family conflict. One is to define different responsibilities clearly and with minimum overlap, and assign them according to personal capabilities and interests. In every well-managed family business I have observed, this approach has been used. On the other hand, in family businesses plagued with conflict, siblings typically perform similar jobs, competing with each other and vying for attention from parents and other family members.

Second, fight issues, not emotions. A woman, whose husband entered then quit her father's business, explained: "Two years ago, my husband was determined to make my father see the importance of expanding. After plotting and pushing, he got the ok. But this was the beginning of almost daily confrontations. He and my father began to fight over people hired and money being spent. If they had discussed plans for company expansion rationally, before my husband began working for my father, much of this could have been resolved." [9]

Finally, establish a family council, composed of all family members key to the future of the business: the founder, spouse, and children, as well as other relatives who have a significant interest in the business. [10] Having regular family meetings allows the airing of problems or differences that might otherwise be ignored—but that won't go away. A family council helps establish open communication, understanding and trust. It also serves as a forum for planning the future of the family and the business.

9 M. Crane, "How to Keep Families from Feuding," *INC.*, February 1982.
10 I. Lansberg, "The Succession Conspiracy," *Family Business Review*, Summer 1988.

Final Note

One last suggestion is in order. Becoming involved in a peer network is highly recommended. There are a variety of national and regional organizations for individuals involved in family ventures. Through the Family Firm Institute (Johnstown, New York), you can become affiliated with local professionals and personal support groups. The Young President's Association is geared to presidents of entrepreneurial and family businesses. Other organizations with a family-business focus include the National Family Business Council and the Small Business Association of New England.

Whatever issues you and a parent or other family business member might be struggling with, it is likely that others have confronted it, or know someone who has. Sharing experiences can be useful and therapeutic for people involved in family ventures.

13

The Image of the American Entrepreneur

The United States, now as in the past, has been seen as the land of opportunity. Both abroad and at home, the United States is seen as providing an inviting and nurturing climate for those wishing to start their own enterprises and reap the rewards. In part, this is because the federal government has encouraged, to a greater degree than in any other country, an atmosphere of *laissez-faire*—a hands-off approach toward the regulation of business and commerce.

Even such legislation as antitrust laws, labor laws and the graduated income tax have not hampered the growth of entrepreneurship. These laws were enacted in response to society's changing perceptions of what constituted "ethical" business practices. They had the equally desirable effect of forcing many industries to develop their own codes of ethical practice—in large part because they wished to have the freedom to set their own rules, rather than having rules imposed on them by Congress.

As the ethical climate of business has changed, so has the stereotype of the entrepreneur. The "good" and lasting stereotype is personified by Horatio Alger. The "ruthless" stereotypes grew out of the unfettered economic activity in the nineteenth century, the era of the robber barons, involving acts of industrial sabotage which today we would not condone, though at the time they were regarded as necessary ingredients for success. The battles of Hill and Harriman over the rights of railroads, the alleged sabotage by John D. Rockefeller of his competitors' oil refineries, the exploitation of child labor in New England's textile mills, and of black labor in the southern cotton plantations, the promoters of "snake oil" and Lydia Pinkham's tonics, leave an unsavory aftertaste in the minds of today's more ethical entrepreneurs. For those who judge in hindsight, "entrepreneurs" may still connote a ruthless, scheming group located a good deal lower than the angels.

Yet, our standards were not their standards—and certain American entrepreneurs have given back to society at least as much as they have profited from it, even before the concepts of social consciousness and business ethics were a glimmer in the business eye of America. Regardless of their motivations—social or *noblesse oblige*, practical "What can you do with 300 million dollars?" or humanitarian "Do unto others ..."—many entrepreneurs gave as good as they got. We have, for instance, the Morgan Library, the Rockefeller Foundation, the Ford Foundation—and the extraordinary legacy of Andrew Carnegie.

In retrospect, Carnegie's case is one of the most interesting, because he described his total change of attitude after amassing his fortune. The son of a Scots handloom weaver, he was able personally to amass $300 million (several billions in today's dollars) in the production of crude steel between 1873 and 1901. He later said, "The fact that this talent for organization and management is rare among men, is proved by the fact that it invariably secures enormous rewards for its possessor." He felt that the law of competition "insures the survival of the fittest in every department." [1]

---

1 Andrew Carnegie, *The Gospel of Wealth*, The Century Co., 1900, pp. 619-20.

(So apparently satisfied was Carnegie with his self-estimate that he did not try to reconcile it with a protective tariff equal to over half the production price of each ton of steel rails.   British steel mills producing rails were thus effectively excluded from the U.S. markets.)

That Carnegie's mind was not easy over his fortune, however, is evident from his statement that "I would as soon give my son a curse as the almighty dollar."   After 1901, when he sold Carnegie Steel to U. S. Steel under pressure from a combine headed by J. P. Morgan, Carnegie personally supervised the giving of more than $300 million in the United States and Great Britain.   Among his gifts to humanity were nearly 3,000 libraries, an Endowment for International Peace, and the Carnegie Institute of Pittsburgh.

From today's perspective, these ancestral entrepreneurs might be described as acting in enlightened self-interest. However, when the same sort of entrepreneurial generosity is demonstrated today by such people as Armand Hammer and An Wang, we are more likely to speak of their acts of philanthropy as fulfilling their social contract.

The implications for today's entrepreneurs of this legacy are several. They include

• An appreciation of new windows of opportunity which are continually opening in the United States, regardless of government regulation.

• An appreciation of how "situational" ethical standards change over time, making judgments about history's "bad guys" suspect.

• The realization that the American entrepreneurial tradition has often included a valuable series of gifts to society, over and above the jobs the entrepreneurs have provided and the goods and services they have supplied.

And yet, a touch of suspicion still tinges entrepreneurial activity. As recently as December 15, 1975, *Time* magazine suggested that a businessman might make the best qualified candidate for president, but noted the "deep-rooted American suspicion of businessmen's motives." Quoting John T. Conner, Chairman of Allied Chemical Corporation and former head of Merck and Co., they added that, "Anyone with previous business experience becomes immediately suspect. Certain segments think he can't make a decision in the public interest."

As an entrepreneur, the most effective way to counter that type of negative thinking is to be aware of your own ethical attitudes, and to build a long-term reputation for integrity and square dealing.

14

Personal Ethics
and the Entrepreneur

Personal ethics provide the guidance and directional control system for human behavior. They govern not only the direction but also the intensity of feeling and emotion during the decision process. They involve internalized beliefs about what is right and what is wrong, and these beliefs differ from individual to individual. Ethics and values thus greatly influence individual decisions. Further, personal ethics do have a considerable impact on relationships with team members, directors, and investors. Because ethics are very personal and internalized, we may not even be aware of them until we are forced into working out tough decisions under pressure.

History, philosophy, and research about the changing and situational nature of business ethics provides a context for thinking about ethical behavior. Asking you below to make decisions involving ethical choices will help you see more clearly the importance of ethical awareness in the career of a successful entrepreneur. Examining the implications of these ethical decisions can help you identify the impact they might have upon you, the entrepreneur, your partners, your customers and your competitors.

Entrepreneurial Decisions

The following questions consider a number of situations; each situation has four possible decisions. Select the one that most closely represents the decision you feel you would make personally. Not all the background information on each question is supplied. Instead, you should make whatever assumptions you feel you would make if you were confronted with these decisions in real life.

1. *You are on a marketing trip for your new venture, calling on the purchasing agent of a major prospective client. Your company is manufacturing an electronic system that you hope the purchasing agent will buy. During the course of your conversation you notice on the cluttered desk of the purchasing agent several copies of a cost proposal for a system from one of your direct competitors. This purchasing agent has previously reported mislaying several of your own company's proposals and asked for additional copies. The purchasing agent leaves the room momentarily to get you a cup of coffee, leaving you alone with your competitor's proposals less than an arm's length away. What would you do?*

___ I do nothing but await the man's return.
___ I sneak a quick peek at the proposal looking for bottom-line numbers.
___ I put a copy of the proposal in my briefcase.
___ I wait until the man returns and ask his permission to see a copy.

2. *You are the co-founder and president of a new venture, manufacturing products for the recreational market. Five months after you launch the business, one of your suppliers notifies you that they will no longer supply you with a critical raw material since you are not a large-volume buyer. Without the raw material you will go out of business. Which of the following would you do?*

___ I would persuade an alternative supplier to fill my needs, even though this will mean they will no longer be able to supply another, noncompeting small manufacturer, who may thus be forced out of business.

__ I am aware of a sizable stockpile of the raw material at another firm (noncompeting) which I can steal. I steal it.

__ I believe that the supplier could be "persuaded" to meet my needs but this would necessitate a sizable under-the-table payoff. I make the payoff.

__ In order to secure the raw material from another supplier who also requires that I be a much larger customer, I would grossly overstate my requirements.

3. *Your small manufacturing company is in serious financial difficulty. A large order of your products is ready to be delivered to a key customer when you discover that the product is simply not right. It will not meet all performance specifications, will cause problems for your customer, and will require rework in the field; but this, you know, will not become evident until after the customer has received and paid for your order. If you do not ship the order and receive the payment as expected your business may be forced into bankruptcy. And if you delay the shipment or inform the customer of these problems you may lose the order, and also go bankrupt. What would you do?*

__ I would not ship the order and place my firm in voluntary bankruptcy.

__ I would inform the customer and declare voluntary bankruptcy.

__ I would ship the order, and inform the customer after I received payment.

__ I would ship the order and not inform the customer.

In the real world, of course, other creative solutions to these situations can be envisioned which were not included here. You were only answering the question, "What would you do?" You were not being asked to do it. Between the intent and the action lies a large gap, which can only be filled by confronting and acting in a number of ambiguous situations.

An awareness of the difference in reactions to "what is ethical" may help you to understand why some aspects of venture creation go wrong for no apparent reason. For example, partnerships dissolve for a myriad of reasons, but differences in ethics are often prime contributors to the breakup. And evidence of shady practices on the part of an entrepreneur who has compromised ethics for a short-term gain is a red flag to an experienced investor. An entrepreneur who is rigidly moralistic in a situation which calls for a flexible attitude is also unlikely to attract investors.

On the other hand, an inexperienced and naive entrepreneur may not understand the operating nuances prevalent in his field of business, and may find that his personal views of "right" and "wrong" simply do not correspond to the rules observed by his competitors. Understanding the limits of a gray area and how to operate within it can be critical to the success of a venture—and it takes both experience and sensitivity to tread the line between savvy and shady.

The Ethical Continuum

One interesting way of examining the question of personal ethics and values is by considering a continuum of the ethical behaviors that can be found in the business world. These behaviors range from the highly rigid and moralistic to the situational and flexible. Moralistic ethics reflect a rigid and independent code of conduct applied uniformly, regardless of different conditions and circumstances. Situational conduct and behavior is influenced mainly by the needs and demands of the situation rather than by some rigid external code. Amoral or illegal conduct and behavior is determined without regard for legal or moral constraints.

Illegal practices—deception, fraud, unfair lending, and so on—are, of course, dealt with by various aspects of the law. The point here is to enable you to test the limits of your own ethical views, not to encourage or condone amoral or illegal practices. More objectively, a moderate risk taker will tend to avoid any behavior that is perceived as too risky.

What is Ethics in Business?

Over a decade ago, a businessman wrote a provocative article asserting that the ethics of business were not those of society but rather those of the poker game. [1] Both strategies, he argued, required intimate knowledge of the rules, insight into the psychology of the other players, a bold front, a considerable amount of self-discipline, and an ability to respond swiftly and effectively to opportunities provided by chance.

"Poker, like business," he continued, "does not allow cheating or unethical behavior such as trying to get your opponents drunk. Poker's own brand of ethics is different from the ethical ideals of civilized human relationships. The game calls for distrust of the other fellow. It ignores the claim of friendship. Cunning deception and concealment of strength and intentions, not kindness and openheartedness, are vital in poker. No one thinks any the worse of poker on that account. And no one should think any the worse of the game of business because its standards of right and wrong differ from the prevailing traditions of morality in our society."

1 Albert Z. Carr, "Is Business Bluffing Ethical?" *Harvard Business Review*, Jan-Feb 1968, pp. 145-52.

However, the author's analogy led him to an uncomfortable conclusion: "That most businessmen are not indifferent to ethics in their private lives, everyone will agree. My point is that in their office lives they cease to be private citizens; they become game players who must be guided by a somewhat different set of ethical standards."

An executive's family life can easily be dislocated if he fails to make a sharp distinction between the ethical systems of the home and the office—or if his wife does not grasp that distinction. Many a businessman who has remarked to his wife, "I had to let Jones go today" or "I had to admit to the boss that Jim has been goofing off lately," has been met with an indignant protest. "How could you do a thing like that? You know Jones is over 50 and will have a lot of trouble getting another job." Or, "You did that to Jim? With his wife ill and all the worry she's been having with the kids?"

This wife saw the problem in terms of moral obligation as conceived in private life; her husband saw it as a matter of game strategy. As a player in a weak position, he felt that he could not afford to indulge an ethical sentiment that might have cost him his seat at the table.

As you might suspect, the article provoked a storm of responses by business people who insisted that *their* business ethics were "ethical," and castigated the author for giving businessmen a bad name. Nonetheless, the author makes a valid point: personal ethics and business ethics are often not in harmony, and either by negotiation or compromise, a resolution must be reached.

"Strategic Misrepresentation" or Lying?

Another real-life furor about ethics occurred not long ago when *The Wall Street Journal* (Jan. 15, 1979) reported on Professor Howard Raiffa's "Competitive Decision-Making" course at the Harvard Business School. During simulated negotiating sessions, students are encouraged to try any tactics at all in order to "win." Lies, which Raiffa termed "strategic misrepresentations," were permissible tactics; Raiffa stated that "in strategic negotiations ... it is unfortunately not always true that complete, unadorned open honesty is the best policy."

Again, the protest mail poured in. Comments were elicited from several dozen CEOs and professors of business, as well as leaders of the Girl Scouts and Boy Scouts. Many of the replies were in defense of this or that corporation's ethical standards and ethical conduct, and many were moralistic in tone. As Sloan K. Childers, vice-president of Phillips Petroleum, wrote:

"Even though lying may be categorized as 'strategic misrepresentation' it is still lying, and Phillips Petroleum Company does not condone or permit such activity in its operations. The course instructor states that in strategic negotiations it is unfortunately not always true that complete honesty is the best policy. We neither agree with this statement nor permit its implications to be applied by our people. It is our opinion that in business, as in other situations, honesty is always the best policy. I recognize that there are many honest differences of view; however, we do not subscribe to that statement that lying is now an acceptable part of negotiations." [2]

To view the controversy in either/or terms of lying versus telling the truth is to skirt the ethical issues which the negotiating process involves, which was the purpose of Raiffa's course. A more thoughtful appreciation of the

2 Leonard H. Orr, ed., "Is Dishonesty Good For Business?" *Business & Society Review*, Summer 1979, pp. 4-19.

ethical issues was presented by Richard N. Rosett, then dean of the University of Chicago Business School. He wrote:

"In bargaining there often are facts that even the most ethical negotiator will conceal; facts that bear on the strength or weakness of his own position are an example. For this reason, and others, sunshine has proved less attractive in practice than its promise. As to Professor Raiffa's course and the account of it that appeared in *The Wall Street Journal*, I can comment only that newspaper writing does not lend itself readily to expression of subtle or complex ideas. Slightly rearranged, the facts of the article are: in artificially simple, one-time negotiations, students learn that dishonesty may pay; in complicated, repeated negotiations of the sort Harvard graduates often engage in, they learn that honesty often pays better. That lesson would have excited little attention, and consequently would likely not have appeared in *The Wall Street Journal*.

"One great advantage of competition is that it provides powerful incentives for ethical behavior even among individuals not so inclined. I have noticed that most businessmen are far less likely to arouse expectations and then not fulfill them than politicians, journalists, clergymen, or university professors." (Ibid.)

An Example of Integrity

Imagine the following situation. You are just 27 years of age and have joined a new mini-computer software firm whose sales this year will reach $1.5 million. Your principal goal as Vice President of International Marketing is to establish profitable distribution for your products in the major industrialized nations. Your stock incentives and highly leveraged bonus plan places clear emphasis on profitability, rather than volume.

In one European country you have narrowed your choice of

distributors to one, from a field of over twenty. It is a top firm, with an excellent track record and management. The chemistry between your team and theirs is right. In fact, they are most anxious to do business with you. The normal royalty you pay is about 15%, but they are so anxious to have your line that they have made it very clear they would be willing to accept the deal for as little as a 10% commission. The other terms of the deal are acceptable to both parties. What do you do?

In this actual situation, the young vice president decided to give them the full 15%, in spite of the fact that they would have settled for much less. In describing his reasoning, he said his main goal was, "... to create a sense of long-term integrity with them. I knew what it would take for them to succeed in gaining the kind of market penetration we were after. I also knew that the economics of their business definitely needed the larger margins from the 15%, rather than the smaller royalty.

"So I figured that if I offered them the full royalty, they would realize I was on their side, and that would create such goodwill that when we did have some serious problems down the road—and you always have them—then we would be able to work together to solve them. And that's exactly what happened. If I had exploited their eagerness to be our distributor, then it only would have come back to haunt me later on."

For the record, this approach was apparently quite successful. In five years this international division grew from zero to $18 million in very profitable sales, and the venture was later acquired by a large firm for $80 million. Equally revealing, now—nearly ten years later—this "young vp" is president of a quite successful software firm backed by leading venture capitalists.

An Entrepreneurial Approach to Ethics

The creative, active and energetic nature of the entrepreneur equips him or her well to cope with ethical dilemmas. This may raise a few eyebrows, even from practicing
entrepreneurs. You can imagine their responses:

"How can we think about ethics when we haven't
enough time to even think about running our venture?"

"Entrepreneurs are doers, not thinkers—and ethics is too
abstract a concept to have any bearing on business realities."

"When you're struggling to survive, you're not worried
about the means you use—you're fighting for one thing:
survival."

To these can be answered: "The contemplation of ethical
behavior is not unlike poetry—emotion recollected in tranquility." This chapter is intended to provide one such tran-
quil opportunity. You have been asked to make decisions in
ethically ambiguous situations, and you have had a chance to
become more aware of your own set of ethics and how they
can be affected by the ethical climate in which you were
forced to make the decision.

During your entrepreneurial career, you will have to act
in the heat of the moment, but later you must find the
energy to recollect, "It didn't feel right," or, contrarily, "I
couldn't have lived with myself if I had done other than
what I did." You will continue to gain insight into your own
ethical values and to identify the limits to which your
tolerance can be stretched.

In the final analysis, ethics and values are very personal
things. As a way to cope with the inevitable conflicts you
will encounter, a first step is developing an awareness of
your own explicit and implicit ethical beliefs and of the
milieu within which you must compete for survival. An

appreciation of this state of affairs is succinctly stated by Fred T. Allen, Chairman and President of Pitney-Bowes, Inc.:

"As businessmen we must learn to weigh short-term interests against long-term possibilities. We must learn to sacrifice what is immediate, what is expedient, if the moral price is too high. What we stand to gain is precious little compared to what we can ultimately lose." (Letter to the Editor, *The Wall Street Journal*, October 17, 1975.)

15

The Entrepreneur
and the Law

When is it ethical to break a law? This is a question as old as law itself. From the beginnings of recorded history, in Egypt and the Middle East, a "code of laws" was always accompanied by a human "interpreter of laws," a judge, to decide when breaking the letter of the law did not violate the spirit or situation which the law was intended to cover. Great moments in history, religion, philosophy and literature focus on the legal/ethical dilemma, and debating teams would wither away if the dilemma were to disappear. Nonetheless, it is a dilemma of a very serious nature for a practicing entrepreneur, and one which—depending on the entrepreneur's actions—can make or break a career.

A small rental service business recently merged with a middle-sized conglomerate. One of the partners in the rental firm had, shortly before the merger, become involved in a severe automobile accident, suffering multiple injuries. Seemingly able to return to work, he still knew that the outlook for his health in the immediate future was unpredictable, due to possible aftereffects of the injuries.

Under these circumstances, he was eager, for the sake of his family and dependent parents, to sell some of the stock acquired in the merger. However, federal law does not allow quick profit-taking from mergers, and therefore would not allow such a sale. The man consulted the president and officers of the larger company. They acquiesced in his plans to sell portions of his stock and stated their conviction that no adverse effect on the stock would result.

Still unsure, the man then checked with his lawyer. The federal law in question, he found, had almost never been prosecuted. Having ascertained the risk, and having probed the rationale of the law as it applied to his case, the man then sold some of the stock acquired in the merger, in order to secure his family in the possible event of his incapacitation or death. (He subsequently recovered completely, which he could not have foreseen.)

In this instance, the individual was balancing the ethical imperatives of family against those of the law. He decided that the intrinsic purpose of the law allowed him to act as he did. In addition, he made as thorough a check as possible of the risks involved.

There are also increasingly frequent situations where one law directly conflicts with another.

A small business investment company in New York City fell into serious financial trouble. The Small Business Administration stated that the company should begin to liquidate its investments, because it would otherwise be in defiance of its agreement with SBA. However, the Securities and Exchange Commission decreed that liquidation would constitute unfair treatment of stockholders. After a year and a half of agonizing negotiation, the company was able to satisfy all the parties, but compromises had to be made on both sides.

A second example of conflicting legal demands involves the Civil Service Code, introduced in the last century to curb patronage abuses in public service. It requires that a civil service test be the basis of hiring. Recently, however, the social goal of encouraging and aiding minorities has led to fair employment acts which require the same public agencies to hire in a non-prejudicial manner, which can conflict with test results. Obviously, both these laws are based on valid ethical intent. But the resolution of such conflicts is no simple matter.

Another arena of legal conflict is international. Unlike the international laws governing commercial airline transportation, there is no international code of business ethics. When doing business abroad, entrepreneurs may find that those with whom they wish to do business have little in common with their own activities: no common language, no common historical context for conducting business, and no common set of ethical beliefs about right and wrong and everything in between.

In the United States, bribing a high official to obtain a favor is considered both ethically and legally unacceptable; in parts of the Middle East, it is the only way to get things done. What we see as a "bribe" others see as akin to a "tip," what you give the headwaiter at a popular restaurant for a good table. But before you too readily assume that one must "when in Rome, do as the Romans do," consider the following:

An American entrepreneur I shall call Hal has owned and operated a sizeable, multi-million-dollar business in Ecuador for nearly twenty-five years. How many times do you suppose he has been approached for bribes by various officials? It come as a surprise to learn that he has never paid a bribe. He puts it this way: "I simply said 'no' from the outset, and they quit coming around!"

What is the entrepreneur to do? Following local practice is one approach. Consulting a lawyer with expertise in international business is another. And assuming that the object of your international business venture is to make money, you must figure out some way which is legally tolerable under the codes of laws which apply, and ethically tolerable to you the entrepreneur.

When Do the Ends Justify the Means?

A central question in any ethical discussion concerns the extent to which a noble end may justify ignoble means, or whether using unethical means for assumed ethical ends may not subvert the aim in some way.

Consider the case of a university agricultural extension service, whose goal is to aid small farmers to increase their crop productivity. The agency is nonprofit, the end is constructive, and profit-oriented only in that the farmers prosper from better crop yields.

The agency, however, suddenly finds itself in an ethical predicament: to support its funding it is being asked to predict the annual increases in crop yield it can achieve. It is unable to provide performance estimates at the required level of specificity. However, it knows that unless its estimates show substantial increases in crop yields, its funding may be heavily reduced.

The agency feels that overly optimistic predictions are unethical, yet their own objectives are highly ethical. Even the unethical aspects are understandable, and perhaps could be condoned, in the context.

Can there be any completely satisfactory solution to this problem? In this case, the extension service decided, if need be, to fudge the figures. The fact that the funding source finally backed down in its demand ameliorated the immediate problem. But if they had not, what then would have been the danger? Certainly a danger existed that the individuals in the organization, altruistic though their intentions were, would begin to think that falsification was the norm, and would forget that actions that run contrary to one's ethical feelings gradually build a debilitating cynicism.

In a personal sense, a noble end never quite justifies a less noble means. In fact, however, the entrepreneur is seldom allowed the luxury of such considerations. The above example shows how one organization responded to pressure. It is a rough rule that, the tougher and more uncompromising the pressure and tactics, the greater will be the likelihood of responding in kind.

Widening the Entrepreneur's Perspective on Law

In considering the thorny question of legality, it is well to look at not only the authority of the law but also its limitations. Laws are made with the deliberate purpose of ensuring justice. They are therefore ethical in intent and deserve respect. However, laws are made by people. Laws do not anticipate new conditions; they do not always have the effect intended; they are sometimes in conflict; and as they stand, they cannot sort out multiple ethical considerations—especially ones at war. Walter Wriston, former chairman of Citicorp, the banking giant, once spoke to this point to a group of executives. He observed that if all the laws of the State of New York were enforced, one would be violated at least once every three minutes by every man, woman and child in the state!

The entrepreneur may decide ethical questions that involve obligations on many sides: to customers, employees, stockholders, family, partners, and to himself, or to a combination—and the entrepreneur's relations with his partners is of primary importance.

An unquestioning reliance on legality is inadequate in today's world. Obviously, the average entrepreneur will not have time to embark on crusades to improve every unintelligent law that is encountered. But the entrepreneur is considered to be an action-oriented person, and action is called for every day.

The good Samaritan's intentions are tied to the means of realizing them (and to continual scrutiny to determine whether the good achieved outweighs the bad). It would be unfortunate if the entrepreneur were timid in realizing his potential for combining action with ethical purpose. There is no reason why they should be considered generically opposed and, in fact, they can be natural allies. The entrepreneur, however, can expect no substitute for individual effort and intelligence.

16

Planning and Goal Setting

More than any other, the old saying, "If you don't know where you're going, any path will take you there," captures the rationale for establishing goals. Successful entrepreneurs seem to know this intuitively and go about it as second nature. Some set goals to make a lot of money. Most are goal-oriented in ways that enable them to identify and pursue more and better business opportunities. This often involves setting goals to acquire the skills, know-how, experience and contacts necessary to succeed. Or it may include goals to develop a business plan and raise capital. Think of planning and goal-setting as creating the road map that will guide your visions and dreams toward practical reality.

We've all heard the reasons why *not* to plan: It's out of date as soon as it's written down; no one knows what tomorrow will bring; it's dangerous to commit to uncertainty; you can't predict the future. The list of such rationalizations can be lengthy. So why plan?

There are many reasons why you should plan; here some of the important ones:

• Research shows a close connection between success and planning and setting goals. One of the most striking characteristics of successful entrepreneurs is their attitude toward and use of plans and goals.

• The process is the key to allocating effectively your most precious commodity, time. Knowing what to say "no" to is vital to entrepreneurs, since there are invariably more opportunities and attractive alternatives than there is time to pursue them.

• Planning and goal setting help you to work smarter, rather than simply harder. They help you to come up with a better way. When applied to developing a business plan, for example, they enable you to understand and clarify risks—and devise ways to manage and reduce those risks.

• Planning and goal setting keep you in a "future-oriented" frame of mind. Thinking ahead helps you be alert for and responsive to problems, opportunities, and changes that will affect you.

• They help you develop and update your strategies by testing your ideas and approaches with others.

• Effective planning and goal setting have a beneficial effect on your motivation and level of effort. Any goal requires some degree of effort to attain it. A goal that is easy means easy going—only a mild level of effort is generated. A goal that is virtually impossible, on the other hand, will dampen the drive to achieve it.

The essential element affecting motivation is how individuals *feel* about their goals. Both too easy and impossible goals create feelings that act against the desire to achieve. The individual pursuing a challenging but attainable goal is highly motivated to work toward that goal.

• Planning and goal setting also give you a "results orientation"—a concern for accomplishment and progress. Once you have stated a specific and measurable goal it will be much easier for you and others to evaluate your performance. It will enable you to see how close you come to achieving it. That means taking responsibility for your actions.

• Planning helps you to manage the risks and uncertainties of the future, but does not predict the future.

• The skill and judgment needed to establish realistic goals can be effective in actually managing and coping with the stressful role of entrepreneur.

Disadvantages of Planning

Planning is neither a panacea nor a sedative. Certain risks and limitations must be noted. [1]

• The cautious person who is anxious about failure may find that setting goals creates a further source of tension and pressure and a heightened fear of failure. The possible mental and physical consequences of such anxiety-inducing activities can be counter productive.

• Establishing goals and plans requires making choices and commitments. It means setting priorities. Inherent in this process is the possibility that future, unknown and better opportunities may be lost or excluded. This dilemma is central to the decision to commit to a course of action that may take a few years to alter or undo.

• For the person who is inclined to be a compulsive and obsessive competitor and achiever, goal setting may have the effect of adding gasoline to the fire. Such a person may focus on a particular task, project, or career to the exclusion of family, friends, community, or other responsibilities. This dilemma faces not only aspiring entrepreneurs but anyone pursuing a highly competitive and demanding career.

• During the demanding early survival stages of a new company, whose life expectancy at times may be estimated in weeks or months, a major allocation of time and effort to planning for next year does not make sense.

Post-Planning Syndrome

We all are familiar with the concept of a learning curve. Its slope is steepest during early mastery of a new task, gradually levels off, and may stabilize or decline. Education

---

1 For a useful discussion of this issue, see David R. Hampton, "The Planning-Motivation Dilemma," *Business Horizons*, vol. 26, no. 3, June 1973.

researchers have discovered that several weeks or a few months following a particular training program, participants often return to their old ways of doing things. Changed behavior in these instances has not been long lasting.

Many of us have heard of or observed—or been victims of—the recent graduate of an intensive management seminar. The first few days back on the job are characterized by great enthusiasm, a new array of buzz words, a prominently displayed coursebook, and graduation plaque on the desk or wall, and exclamations of "We need to (or will) do things differently around here from now on!"

The seasoned greeter of this new behavior knows that the recent graduate will probably need a week or two to get all of this out of his system, to calm down a bit, and to return to normalcy. Knowing that this enthusiasm and exhortation is not likely to endure, he is receptive—at least verbally—and patient.

By the second Monday after the return, the fever has receded to a moderate level: the end is in sight! The routine, occasional tranquility, and predictable crises of old will soon return.

The same thing happens in the post-planning syndrome. The plan did not work, so we fall back on *activity-oriented* routine, or crisis management. This routine is counter productive because it lacks or confuses priorities, has no longer-term purpose, and isn't aimed at attaining particular objectives. How many times, for example, has someone returned from a day at the office saying, "I was busy all day but I didn't get a thing done"?

Why Plans Fail

Perhaps there is no greater frustration for entrepreneurs and managers than to experience failure with plans seemingly well prepared and well intended. Not only is it frustrating—well prepared plans consume many precious hours—it is downright demoralizing when the plan doesn't work. This failure in turn breeds contempt for the process of planning, particularly when success has been realized without it.

What are the behaviors that seem to contribute to planning failure, and what must be done to reduce the possibility of failure? Simply working harder is not enough. Working smarter is essential. Working smarter entails awareness of six basic reasons why plans fail.

No Real Goal. Many people aren't aware of what a goal is. They may allude to some admirable mission such as "improved performance," "growth," or "increased sales," but these vagaries are better labeled fantasies than goals. A goal must be concrete. If goals are not specific, measurable, and realistic, the plan is unlikely to work. What is the definable end result?

Failure to Anticipate Obstacles. Entrepreneurs who deliberately identify potential obstacles and how to overcome them have superior batting averages for their plans. They break down large obstacles into small hurdles, and then establish action steps to overcome them. A plan must be flexible and must recognize and provide solutions to the anticipated obstacles if it is to deal with the unknown and unexpected.

Lack of Progress Reviews. Plans that fail often have no progress review dates, or they are allowed to slip by. Periodic reviews alert you to any need for reassessment. Milestones provide an important sense of accomplishment, and motivation to succeed further.

However, experienced practitioners know that excessive detail and analysis in the review process can slow down goal accomplishment. The whole process must be kept simple.

Effective progress reviews simply test the velocity, direction, and reality of the plan. "Where are we going?" and "How are we doing?" are two central questions to ask constantly.

Lack of Commitment. Personal commitment is critical to the success of any plan. Unless the people who must implement a plan are committed to it, the goals of the plan are not likely to be met. Commitment also means focus: the need to zero in on the goal, and to say "no" to other attractive alternatives. Commitment stems from involvement in the process of developing goals. Involving subordinates or co-workers in the process stimulates their interest, input, and more importantly, their feelings of ownership in the plan.

Discussion that involves negotiating, compromising, and data sharing helps to arrive at goals that are jointly established. Otherwise, when a plan doesn't work, it's easy to say, "I told you so; it wasn't my plan!" Collaboration is essential to gaining commitment to a plan.

For the determined entrepreneur, another dilemma is over-commitment. By blocking out important feedback, it can lead to ignoring reality and pressing ahead on a course that is unduly risky and may result in costly failure.

Failure to Revise Goals. An even surer way to torpedo the best-laid plan is not to reassess and reset goals and plans as realities unfold. By definition entrepreneurs live with turbulence, constant change and uncertainty. New competition, loss of key personnel, overly ambitious timetables, and a host of other uncertainties rear their ugly heads as planned action goes along. Inflexibility in the face of these matters forces adherence to an unworkable plan. Failure is built into a plan that does not respond to changes in the environment, internal and external. Failing to revise goals when appropriate is to ignore reality. This is a key aspect of the *process* of planning and goal setting.

Failure to Learn from Experience. Entrepreneurs may do the right things, yet fail if they don't learn from what they are doing. They will ignore feedback—"we're on schedule but our budget is running over"—or deny that it is even happening—"go back and check your figures!" Failure to learn from current and past experience seems to stem from an unwillingness to change a way of doing things, or a refusal to accept failure. There is comfort in the thought, "It's worked before, it must be right." But failing to be a proactive learner will prohibit this kind of entrepreneur from ever finding out that things are not right until it is too late. Flexibility is a must for launching a successful new venture.

Effective Goal Setting

The goals set by successful entrepreneurs are not dreams, fantasies or the product of wishful thinking. Nor are they mere predictions or guesses about future outcomes. A goal is far more concrete and specific—it is a decision or choice about future outcomes. Goals translate visions to reality.

Planning and goal setting is a *process* for managing uncertainties and minimizing risks, *not* for forecasting the future. It is the process by which you plan where you want to go, how fast, how to get there, and what to do along the way. It also defines performance so that you can assess progress.

Reassessing and resetting goals and plans periodically is an integral part of this process. Plans should be *goal-oriented* rather than *activity-oriented*, and these two should not be confused.

Planning also can be used to build team commitment. Thus

• Plan with team members whose commitment is critical to success.

• Make performance expectations clear.

- Create a win-win situation for everyone who is critical to success.
- Provide and solicit feedback on progress, in order to maintain commitment and keep plans on track.

Goals properly set to chart future courses must be carefully defined and meet the following criteria:
- A goal must be *specific* and *concrete*, rather than abstract and out of focus.
- A goal must be *measurable*.
- A goal must be *related to time*; that is, it must be specific about what will be accomplished over a certain time period.
- A goal must be *realistic*. Simply meeting the first three criteria is not enough; the goal must be challenging but attainable.

Once set, goals should not become static targets. Goal setting is not a task but a process, a way of dealing with the world. A number of distinct steps are involved in this process; these steps are repeated over and over as conditions change.

Step 1. Establish the goal. (It must be specific, measurable, time-related, and attainable.)

Step 2. Set priorities (from most to least important goals and action steps); identify potential goal conflicts and trade-offs and how these can be resolved.

Step 3. Identify potential problems and obstacles that could prevent you from attaining your goal.

Step 4. Specify the tasks and action steps that must be performed to accomplish the goal.

Step 5. Indicate how you will measure the results you hope to accomplish.

Step 6. Establish milestones for reviewing the progress you are making. These should be specific dates on your calendar.

Step 7. Identify the risks involved in meeting your goals and what must be done to avoid high or low chances of success.

Step 8. Identify help and resources that may be needed to obtain your goal.

Step 9. Review progress periodically.

Step 10. Revise goals and plans as feedback and results indicate such revision is appropriate.

These are the basic ingredients of effective goal setting. Research and practical experience have shown that these ingredients are common to almost all successful planning efforts. Become familiar with this process, adapt it to your needs as suitable and practice it. It is through effective goal setting that the lessons learned will be translated into personal goals and action steps. And only effective goal setting can produce an action plan likely to produce a successful venture.

Lastly, it is important to recognize that the *content* and *process* are far more important than the *form*. The plan can be a beautifully written, artistic "success," yet fail. Not surprisingly, there are entrepreneurs who plan in the shower and on the back of an envelope—effectively. But all successful planning seems to have the same ingredients and process in common.

17

Shaping a Personal Strategy

One of the principal aims of this book is to expose you in depth and in breadth to the nature, peculiarities, and realities of the entrepreneur and the entrepreneurial role. At a more practical and personal level it is aimed at helping you to evaluate thoroughly your *attraction* to entrepreneurship and the *fit* between you and the entrepreneurial role and its characteristics.

One experienced investor in small ventures, Louis L. Allen, has this view of the importance of self-selection:

"Unlike the giant firm which has recruiting and selection *experts* to screen the wheat from the chaff, the small business firm, which comprises the most common economic unit in our business system, cannot afford to employ a personnel manager ... . More than that, there's something very special about the selection of the owners: they have selected themselves ... . As I face self-selected top managers across my desk or visit them in their plants or offices I have become more and more impressed with the fact that this self-selection process is far more important to the *success or failure* of the company the man is starting than the monetary aspects of our negotiations."

Finally, no individual has all of the required managerial skills or personal qualities, and the presence or absence of any single dimension does not guarantee success or failure as an entrepreneur. However, knowing that you do not have a certain attribute or skill and knowing where and how to get it, or how to compensate for it, can be as valuable as already having it. One outstanding individual I shall call Chet has worked with over fifty entrepreneurs over the past twenty years, all of whom have built substantial companies from practically nothing, and have become multi-millionaires. His advice on this matter is insightful: "The best entrepreneurs I have worked with have one thing in common: they know what they don't know. If their egos are too big to know that, then they won't succeed."

There is, of course, far more to building a substantial new venture than the behavior and personality of the principal players. How they adapt to changing conditions, and how effectively they complement each other and work together, are at least as important. And silk purses are not made from sows' ears. Unless the opportunity is attractive and attainable, even the very best entrepreneur is unlikely to succeed.

A personal strategy assessment can be viewed as the personal equivalent of a business plan—or like a flight simulator, a great place to test your skills and abilities without risk. It provides an organized framework to help you examine your goals, preferences and aspirations; your track record, both the ups and downs; the key people and events which have shaped your experience to date; your strengths and weaknesses, and how to overcome the latter through a planned apprenticeship and a judicious choice of teammates.

A systematic recording and analysis of your experience can help you see where you have been, and provide some direction on where you need to go—things you can be looking for in the future. In addition, there is growing evidence that awareness of customers, employees and the environment is closely linked to effective entrepreneurship.[1]

Maximizing Self-Assessment

All of us possess various personal frames of reference, assumptions, values, and stereotypes that shape our self-images which we want to preserve, protect, and, if necessary, defend. These inhibitions are an obstacle to accurate and useful self-assessment.

One way to grapple with this problem is to have a framework for looking at what is likely to take place, and some guidelines for giving feedback to and receiving feedback from others. The Johari Window is one conceptual scheme for this process.

The Johari Window

	Known to Self	Not Known to Self
Known to Others (partners, investors)	Open area (shared opinions)	Blind area (need to know)
Not Known to Others	Hidden area (unshared)	Unknown area (unconscious)

Named after Joe Luft and Harry Ingraham; from D. A. Kolb, I. M. Rubin, and J. M. McIntyre, *Organizational Psychology: An Experiential Approach*, 2d ed., Prentice-Hall, 1974.

1 Harry Schrage, "The R&D Entrepreneur: Profile of Success," *Harvard Business Review*, vol. 43, No. 6, Nov-Dec 1965.

Most of us can think about examples for ourselves for boxes 1 and 3 (the open and hidden areas), and we can think of blind areas (2) for others, but of course the unknown area (4) is exactly that.

One of the primary benefits of self-assessment is in helping ourselves to identify blind spots that could be costly, and to examine more carefully some previously hidden assumptions.

Assessing Entrepreneurial Roots

One useful way to start assessing yourself and your career is to think about your own preferences in terms of life-style and work. Couple this with a look into the future: what you would like most to be doing and how you would like to live? Give thought to the following questions.

• What gives you energy? What would are the activities or conditions—both work and non-work—under which you find the greatest amount of personal energy, satisfaction and sense of enjoyment? For example, these could be such things as selling something, going fishing, working on a problem, or traveling. These are the things you enjoy doing the most, and that energize you. What is it about them that really motivates you, and why?

• What activities or circumstances create for you the greatest amount of personal dissatisfaction, anxiety, or dis-content? These are the things you enjoy the least, and take away your energy and motivation. Why is this so?

• Think of yourself 20 to 30 years from now. Describe how you think you would like to spend an ideal month. What would your ideal lifestyle and work style be like? In-clude such things as income, involvement in work, family, community, religious or other activities, where and how you would like to live, who your close friends are likely to be, and so on. What is it that attracts and repels you about this ideal existence?

• Think about all the businesses that you could go into. Make a list of the ten businesses you most definitely *would* want to enter, and the ten businesses you most definitely *would not* want to enter. Rank order the lists. Do they share any common attributes? What is it about these that you believe will give you energy and motivation, or take them away?

Now review your responses and reasons why to the questions above. List below those themes, ideas, or characteristics which give you the *most* energy and enjoyment and those that give you the *least* energy or enjoyment.

• List as many as you can of the activities you have attempted on your own. They might include such things as making or building something on your own, having a part- or full-time business of your own (paper route, lawn mowing, auto repairs), a self-financed education or hobby, or finding a job or school on your own. Looking back, what did you learn about yourself, self-employment, managing people and making money?

• List the sports, hobbies, and other activities you have participated in which have an individual rather than a team character (e.g., chess, track, tennis, golf versus football, baseball, basketball). What attracted you to them?

• Have you ever been fired or have you quit a job? Why? What difference has this made?

• Have you ever changed jobs or relocated? What were the circumstances? How did you feel about making such moves? How important is it to you to stay put and have roots?

• List any friends, relatives, or acquaintances who own and operate their own businesses or are self-employed? How do you view them and their business roles? What have you learned from them about self-employment? The things that attract or repel? The trade-offs? The risks and rewards? Entry strategies that work?

• If you have ever started your own business (part- or full-time) of any kind, or worked in a small company, list the things you liked most and least about it.

• How comfortable are you with uncertainty, paradoxes, ambiguity and lack of structure? Would you take a job in which you were 90% sure of a paycheck this month, 70% the next, 50% six months from now, but only 10-20% a year from now? Why?

• If you have ever worked for a larger company (over 500 employees or about $40-50 million in sales), list the things you liked most and least about your work.

Are there any other themes, patterns or thought-pro-vokers which may have emerged as a result of completing your answers to these questions?

Evaluating Your Assessment

What do you find most appealing about being an entre-preneur?

What do you find least attractive about the demands of entrepreneurship, especially during the first few years?

How do the requirements of entrepreneurship— espec-ially early sacrifices, total immersion, work load, and long-term commitment—fit with your own aims, values, and mo-tivations?

What specific conflicts do you anticipate between your aims and values and the demands of entrepreneurship?

What is it about the specific opportunity you want to pursue that will provide you with sustained energy and motivation? How do you know this?

What do you feel are your entrepreneurial strengths and weaknesses with regard to your chosen venture opportunity?

Is your current venture opportunity really for you? Do you want and need partners? What kind? What has to happen now to get the odds of success in your favor?

What action is necessary to fill any relevant gaps in your experience, or to resolve any issues raised so far? How do you plan to do this?

Conclusion

Achieving your entrepreneurial dreams involves converting those dreams to a tangible vision, and motivating yourself and those with you to pursue a doable strategy.

What is most important is the *process* and *discipline* that puts you in charge of evaluating and shaping the choices, and initiating action that makes sense for you, rather than letting it just happen. Having a long-term sense of direction can be highly motivating and extremely helpful in determining what to say "no" to, which is much harder than saying "yes," and can temper opportunism and impulsive hunches with a more thoughtful strategic purpose.

Why is that so important? You are what you do. Today's choices, whether or not they are thought out, become tomorrow's track record and resume. Unthinking opportunism and impulse may end up shaping you in ways that you may not find so attractive ten years hence. What is worse, it may also result in your failing to obtain just those experiences you need in order to have high-quality opportunities come your way later on.

18

Assessing Entrepreneurial Attributes and Roles

How do entrepreneurs think and act? What do they do? While they come in all sizes, shapes and varieties, there are some common themes that emerge after you have got to know a hundred or more of them.

If successful entrepreneurs know what they do and do not know, then sizing up whether you "think and act" like many successful entrepreneurs can be a useful process. You can figure out what attitudes and habits to improve in order to be more entrepreneurial.

What follows will not tell you whether or not you will succeed as an entrepreneur. What it can do is help you to appreciate the mind-set, and to ascertain whether it rings true, or resonates with you. It can also provide clues to mental attitudes and habits you need to strengthen. Further, it can assist in identifying the capabilities of a perspective business partner whose strengths would complement your weaknesses.

Entrepreneurial Attributes

Listed below are a number of attributes which researchers, venture capitalists, and practitioners believe to be important for entrepreneurial success. It is unlikely that any one person is exceptionally strong or weak on all of these dimensions. Respond by placing an X in the appropriate column as you compare yourself with other businessmen and women and entrepreneurs. The most important output of this exercise is an honest, accurate, and realistic assessment of how you measure in each of these dimensions.

Please rank yourself on a 5-1 scale, 5 being the strongest and 1 the weakest.

Total Commitment, Determination and Perseverance: You must give your all; even if means sacrifices in family life, a cut in pay, and an incipient ulcer, in order to succeed.

Drive to Achieve and Grow: Self-starting, growth-minded and self-motivated, using objective measures to keep score.

Opportunity and Goal Oriented: Ability and commitment to set clear goals and objectives that are high and challenging but are realistic and attainable in the pursuit of opportunity.

Taking Initiative and Personal Responsibility: Desire to seek and take initiative and to put yourself in situations where you are personally responsible for the success or failure of the operation; one who takes the initiative to solve problems or fills leadership vacuums and who dislikes situations where one's impact on problems cannot be measured. A self-reliant doer.

Persistent Problem Solving: Intense and determined desire to complete a task or solve a problem; a strong determination to get the job done.

Veridical Awareness and a Sense of Humor: Optimistic realism, knowing weaknesses as well as strengths, knowing what you do and do not know, and the ability to retain a sense of perspective.

Seeking and Using Feedback: Demonstrated capacity to seek and use feedback on your performance in order to know how you are doing, and to take corrective action and to improve.

Internal Locus of Control: The belief that you can make a difference, that your accomplishments as well as failures lie within your personal control and influence, rather than determined by luck or other external, personally uncontrollable events and circumstances.

Tolerance for Ambiguity, Stress and Uncertainty: Able to live with modest to high levels of ambiguity, uncertainty and conflicting paradoxes on a continuous basis. Sufficient self-confidence that job security is not important.

Calculated Risk-Taking and Sharing: Preference for taking moderate, calculated risks; and for not taking risks you do not have to incur.

Low Need for Status and Power: Achievement is the driving force; power and status are by-products of your accomplishments, rather than ends in themselves.

Integrity and Reliability: High personal standards, unwillingness to compromise them, belief that an excellent reputation is key to long-term success.

Decisiveness, Urgency and Patience: Living with the entrepreneur's paradox; balancing the need to get things done with the need to look down the road and take a longer-range view of what needs to be achieved.

Dealing With Failure: Ability to tolerate rejection and to use failures as learning experiences and to better understand your role in causing the failure in order to avoid similar problems in the future.

Team Builder and Hero Maker: The ability to make heroes of the people you attract to the venture, to share control and give credit.

Entrepreneurial Role Requirements: What Does It Take?

In recent years the "iron-man competition" and marathons have become enormously popular for participants and spectators alike. Entrepreneuring can be thought of as a "marathon of life." What is it like? What does it take? How can you be prepared—especially for the "Heartbreak Hills" (referring to an especially punishing series of hills in the late stages of the Boston Marathon)? What follows are some of the principal demands and requirements of being an entrepreneur. The assessment process can help to understand the "race to be run," what it is likely to entail, and what to prepare yourself for.

Listed below are a number of entrepreneurial role requirements which researchers, entrepreneurs, venture capitalists, and practitioners believe to be important for entrepreneurial success. It is unlikely that any one person is exceptionally strong or weak on all of these dimensions, but an entrepreneur should have more strengths than weaknesses, and know which ones are which. Respond by placing an X in the appropriate column as you compare yourself with other business men and women. The most important output of this exercise is an honest, accurate, and realistic assessment of how you stand on each of these requirements.

Please rank yourself on a 5-1 scale, 5 being the strongest and 1 the weakest:

Accommodation to the Venture: Extent to which the entrepreneur's career and venture are treated as the number one priority—above family, community, etc.

Stress Generation: The cost of accommodation, the need to balance the achievements possible under short-term stress with the ability to relax and ease off when necessary.

Economic and Professional Values: Extent to which one believes in and is committed to the conventional economic and financial values of the American system of enterprise, such as profits, capital gains, private ownership, earnings per share, etc.

Ethics: Esteem in which they are held; extent to which one's business conduct tends to be defined and adaptive to the demands and needs of each situation rather than by a rigid code of conduct applied uniformly regardless of different conditions and circumstances.

19

Feedback from Others

A source of very useful information is the impressions of people who know us well. Finding out what your colleagues feel are your strengths and weaknesses depends on how long the person has known you, the degree of rapport that exists, and what that person knows about you—your business skills (management skills) and your personal characteristics (entrepreneurial attributes). Rarely, however, does this information get shared.

Seeking Outside Feedback

To expand your sources of feedback, go to outside peers, potential partners and professionals, and enlist their impressions of how they perceive your entrepreneurial strengths and weaknesses. Here are some issues for you to consider that provide some guidance in obtaining outside feedback.

• Consider the context in which the person knows you. A business colleague may be better able to comment upon your managerial skills. Your partners in a new venture project are excellent potential sources of feedback. A personal friend may be able to comment on your motivations or on how your family will be affected by your deciding to become an entrepreneur. Your spouse, if you are married, is obviously an excellent source of data on the latter.

• Chat with the person *before* asking him or her to provide any written impressions, and indicate the areas you think he or she can best comment upon. One way to do this is to formulate your own questions first. For example, "I've been asking myself the following question ... I would really like your impressions."

• Encourage the person to describe specific situations or behaviors that have influenced his impressions of you.

• The writing of impressions is important for several reasons: The person can take some time to think about the issues after you have spoken with him or her—they needn't be "off-the-top" ideas. Recording them on paper will help you in the future as you pull together all of your experiences and continue to think more specifically about your potential as an entrepreneur.

Receiving Feedback

Receiving feedback from others, whether you know them well or not at all, can be a trying experience. The following guidelines, while not all-inclusive, can facilitate the process.

• Avoid becoming defensive, by not taking negative comments in a personal way.

• Listen carefully to what is being said and think about it. Avoid answering or debating, or rationalizing as to why your opinion may differ. You'll have plenty of time for that later. Think it over first.

• Ask for specific comments in areas which you may feel are particularly important to you personally and to the success of the venture. Probe for more detail if you are not sure what the feedback says. Paraphrase what you think you heard to check your perception, and by asking the other person if that was, in fact, what they wanted to say.

• Ask for help in identifying possible implications of the self-assessment data. Don't worry about reaching final conclusions or decisions. At no point will you arrive at any clean go/no-go appraisal—it just isn't that simple. The process is cumulative, and what you do about weaknesses, for example, is far more important than what the particular weaknesses might be. After all, we all have weaknesses.

• Be honest and straightforward in these discussions. Time is too precious and the road to new venture success too slippery to clutter it with game playing or hidden agendas.

• Seek others within and outside the session to cross-check feedback you have received, and to supplement the session-generated data. This will confirm or deny the accuracy of the feedback.

A Feedback Checklist

A suggested feedback checklist is provided below. Feel free to make any additions to the forms that seem appropriate. After explaining why you are asking the person to do this, and what you would like them to focus on, leave a copy of the checklist with them to complete and return to you.

They can either mail or deliver their responses to you. How you do this may depend on your decision concerning anonymity. Ideally, you should have them a few days in order to personally reflect on their content and implications.

How many people you approach for all forms is obviously up to you. The greater the number and the wider the range of their perspectives, the more potential value this exercise will be to you. You should remember that what you say during the preliminary chat with each person will *help him* considerably to provide impressions that will *help you.*

FEEDBACK GUIDE

Part I—Strengths and Weaknesses

1. What are the areas—as an entrepreneur, relevant experience, management know-how—that you see as my greatest potential or existing strengths in terms of the venture opportunity we have discussed?

2. What specific situations led you to indicate these as areas of strength?

3. What are the one or more areas—as an entrepreneur, relevant experience, management know-how—that you see as my greatest potential or existing weaknesses in terms of succeeding in the specific venture opportunity we have discussed?

4. What specific situations lead you to indicate these as areas of weakness?

5. Record below any suggestions or "prescriptions" you could offer that would be helpful for me to consider.

6. Given my venture opportunity, what is your evaluation of my partners? (This assumes you know them, even if casually or in a limited way.) Do they have the relevant experience, know-how and management competencies to implement my own?

7. Given my venture opportunity, and based on your evaluation of my weaknesses, should I consider any additional members for my management team, and what should be their strengths and relevant experience?

Part II—Entrepreneurial Attributes

Please rate your impressions of my entrepreneurial attributes.

Very Strong/Adequate/
A Question/Real Weakness/No Basis to Judge

a. Total Commitment, Determination and Perseverance
b. Drive to Achieve and Grow
c. Opportunity and Goal Oriented
d. Taking Initiative and Personal Responsibility
e. Persistent Problem-Solving
f. Veridical Awareness and a Sense of Humor
g. Seeking and Using Feedback
   (Gambler—Calculated—Conservative)
h. Internal Locus of Control
i. Tolerance for Ambiguity
j. Calculated Risk-Taking and Sharing
k. Low Need for Status and Power
l. Integrity and Reliability
m. Decisiveness, Urgency and Patience
n. Dealing With Failure
o. Team Builder and Hero Maker
   p. Accommodation to the Venture
   q. Stress Generation
   r. Economic and Professional Values
   s. Ethics
   Comments:

Part III—Management Skills and Competencies

Please rate your impressions of my management skills.

Major Strength/Meets Threshold/
Major Weakness/No Basis for Judgement

1. Marketing Skills
   a. Market Research an Evaluation
   B. Marketing Planning
   C. Product Pricing
   D. Sales Management
   E. Direct Selling
   F. Service
   G. Distribution Management
   H. Product Management
   I. New-Product Planning
2. Operations/Technical Skills
   A. Manufacturing Management
   B. Inventory Control
   C. Cost Analysis and Control
   D. Quality Control
   E. Production Scheduling and Flow
   F. Purchasing
   G. Job Evaluation
3. Financial Skills
   A. Raising Capital
   B. Cash Flow Management
   C. Credit and Collection Management
   D. Short-Term Financing Alternatives
   E. Familiar with Public & Private Stock Offerings
   F. Bookkeeping and Accounting
   G. Specific Skills
       Cash Flow Analysis
       Breakeven Analysis

   Contribution Analysis
   Profit & Loss
   Balance Sheet
4. Micro Computer Skills
 A. Spread Sheet Analysis
 B. Word Processing
 C. Database Access and Use of Electronic Mail
 D. Graphics
5. Administrative Skills
 A. Problem Solving
 B. Communication
 C. Planning
 D. Decision Making
 E. Project Management
 F. Negotiating
 G. Personnel Administration
6. Interpersonal and Team Skills
 A. Leadership and Influence
 B. Listening and Trust Building
 C. Helping
 D. Obtaining and Using Feedback
 E. Conflict Management
 F. Teamwork
 G. Developing Subordinates
 H. Climate and Culture Building
7. Knowledge of Applicable Law
 A. Corporate Law
 B. Contract Law
 C. Patent and Proprietary Rights Laws
 D. Tax Law
 E. Real Estate Law
 F. Investment Agreement Law

Bibliography

GENERAL BACKGROUND AND REFERENCE

New Venture Creation, Third Edition, Jeffry A. Timmons, Irwin, 1989. One of the leading texts for MBA courses on entrepreneurship and new ventures.

Encyclopedia of Small Business Resources, David E. Gumpert and Jeffry A. Timmons, Harper & Row, 1984. (Published in hard cover by Doubleday & Co. in 1982 as *The Insider's Guide to Small Business Resources*.) A topic-by-topic listing of sources for information, consulting help, and capital for new and small enterprise. "This is a competent and comprehensive guide in a field in which information is scattered and hard to come by" (Forbes).

Encyclopedia of Entrepreneurship, edited by Kent, Sexton, and Vesper, Prentice-Hall 1982. A fine collection of research articles by the leading academicians on many aspects of the entrepreneurial process: the entrepreneur, the venture, the environment, the history, the non-academic literature, and suggestions for further research.

Entrepreneurship for the Eighties, Gordon Baty, Prentice-Hall 1981. A breezy, practical walk-through of starting a new venture by someone who has done it.

Frontiers of Entrepreneurship Research: 1981-1988, edited by J. A. Hornaday, J. A. Timmons, and K. H. Vesper et al., Babson College. These volumes include the complete proceedings of annual conferences on entrepreneurship research. The data-based papers cover every aspect of the venture creation process. The authors are from academia, government and the private sector, both in this country and abroad. These documents are the most comprehensive existing compendia of research into entrepreneurship.

Growing Concerns, edited by David Gumpert, Wiley 1984. A compendium of articles about emerging growth ventures from the *Harvard Business Review*.

New Business Ventures and the Entrepreneur, Howard H. Stevenson, Michael J. Roberts, Irving Grousbeck, Irwin 1985. This book, an update and revision of Patrick Liles' 1974 publication bearing the same title, contains cases and technical notes on specific aspects of venture creation.

Trials and Rewards of the Entrepreneur, articles reprinted from the *Harvard Business Review*. These articles, written between 1964 and 1982, deal with various aspects of the emerging, growing and maturing venture. It is nice to have them all under the same cover.

NEWSPAPERS AND PERIODICALS

Timely, often provocative information for and about entrepreneurs can be found in the following publications:

Babson Entrepreneurial Review (Babson College, Babson Park MA 02157)

Harvard Business Review—Growing Concerns (Soldiers Field Road, Boston MA 02163).

Ideas (Ernst & Whinney, Privately Owned and Emerging Businesses, 2000 National City Center, Cleveland OH 44114).

In Business (Box 323, Emmaus PA 18049).

INC. magazine (38 Commercial Wharf, Boston MA 02110).

The New York Times frequently has items of interest to entrepreneurs.

Small Business Reporter (Bank of America, San Francisco CA).

Venture (35 W. 45th Street, New York NY 10036).

The Wall Street Journal publishes a regular feature on small business.

Index

10
LH